INTUITIVE WRITING

THE REMEDY FOR WRITER'S BLOCK AND THE SECRET TO AUTHENTIC COMMUNICATION

JACQUELINE FISCH

Published 2023

Printed in the United States of America

978-1-7365542-3-4 (hardcover)
978-1-7365542-4-1 (paperback)
978-1-7365542-5-8 (ebook)
Library of Congress Control Number: 2023907176

Cover design by Stacey Aaronson
Book design by The Blue Garret

For information or bulk orders, address:
Sovereign Owl Publishing
3702 W. Spruce St. #1008
Tampa, FL 33607
hi@jacquelinefisch.com

To my clients and writing community for your courage to show up to the page.

To you, reader, for sharing your stories, because a story is only powerful when shared.

And of course, to my family, who fully supports me in my writerly adventures.

CONTENTS

PART FOUR
KEEPING ON

INTRO

There's an idea out there that writing is hard. That anyone who writes is tormented, frustrated, and maybe a little wacky. Many professional writers complain at every turn — about the words not showing up, about not having the time — and then groan about everyone outside of them — editors, clients, readers, bosses, and agents. And what they say to and about themselves is far worse — resulting in wasted time, procrastination, overthinking, and missed deadlines.

Those who have to create content for their business get all tangled up writing for an ideal audience, standing out from competitors, digging for the benefits of their offers so they can make sales, and tinkering with the tech behind social media and newsletters.

If you want to be a tormented writer, this book isn't for you. Same goes if you prefer to cling to your stories about writing being painful and frustrating.

If you're here because you're ready to let go of those stories, choose a new path, and write with a lot more ease — I invite you to join me for a journey.

Writing isn't depleting, it's life-giving and energizing.

Anyone who tells you otherwise is projecting. Choose to believe your own story about writing.

Merriam-Webster defines intuition as "the power or faculty of attaining direct knowledge or cognition without evident rational thought and inference."

Intuition is a knowing. It's trusting the knowledge we receive without seeing hard facts. Intuition happens in our bodies, not in our brains. We can't think our way to intuition. We stop forcing and allow. Listening to intuition is a massive trust exercise.

People often mix up the ideas of instinct and intuition. Instinct is an unconscious and automatic response — think breathing, flinching at noises, cringing as a squirrel dashes in front of your car. While intuition is that knowing we can't explain. Things like getting a bad vibe from that weird house on the corner, having a sudden insight into a problem, picking up your phone as your friend is texting you at that very moment.

Intuitive writing is trusting the words that fall out of our fingertips. It's about allowing the words to come through without thinking or forcing — and instead, surrendering. We learn to write what's in our heart that we have been afraid to write — and to write our stories naturally and authentically. Whether it's for a website, a program launch, or a book, when we follow the path of intuitive writing, one thing is sure to happen — we *will* get our words out.

Everything is energy. Words carry significant energy. And how you do writing is how you do life. If you can find ease in the writing process, you can find ease in other areas of your life. Intuitive writing is about embodying pure love — for words on a page, yes, and also for our work, relationships, health, and spirituality.

My last book is called *Unfussy Life,* and as I wrestled with whether to call this book *The Unfussy Writer*, I knew the word "unfussy" had run its course. It would have been the next logical title in my body of work. But "un" means the opposite, and "fussy" is a negative word. Pairing two negative words together doesn't have the high vibe I embody in my writing today.

Unfussy perfectly sums up the journey from chaos to calm. But we're going further here and getting an upgrade — now we're *intuitive.*

Being an intuitive writer means you tend body, mind, and spirit. How you move your body, what you think about when you wake up, who you listen to on social media, and what you put in your mouth will all help you as you put pen to paper.

I'll be your personal writing coach on this journey, and I'm excited to guide you.

My goal: To help you fall in love with your writing — by starting today to take small, imperfect actions without knowing entirely how the finished product will look. And to have a whole lot of fucking fun while doing it.

Who's this well-adjusted author dishing all this writing advice?

Hey, I'm Jacqueline Fisch. Most people call me Jacq (sounds like Jack but spelled fancy and French — neither of which I am). Then there's Jacq-of-all-trades — I am also not that. In fact, I gave the middle finger to my corporate job when a middle manager told me I had to expand my focus beyond writing to learning some boring software in the name of "well-roundedness."

Sometimes I say I'm an intuitive writing coach and founder of The Intuitive Writing School. Sometimes I say I'm a copywriter, author, and copy coach. My clients tell me I'm a mind reader, and so much more than a writer. They call me a miracle worker and life saver. You can decide for yourself. What you call me doesn't really matter.

I wrote this book because I believe that what you're here to say matters. I want to help you — to write more, to write when you're procrastinating, and to start and *finish* those writing projects.

Writing will change your life by helping you hear your inner voice, connecting you to yourself in a noisy world, and offering a safe space to show you where you're going next. And when it does, writing becomes a lifeline — it begins to support you.

We're going to demystify the muse and bust some myths. The healing and transformational tool that is writing isn't reserved only for the elite, the naturally talented, or those with degrees from Ivy League schools. Writing *is* for everyone. I'm sharing this advice with you as someone who did not attend an Ivy League school and had no formal education in writing or editing. I may have been born with a natural ability to write, but I've honed it over thirteen years in the corporate world and almost a decade of writing for myself and others.

I hold a three-year marketing degree from a technical school in Ontario. It wasn't my education (or lack thereof) that opened doors — it was my tenacity and willingness to be visible, take action, play, experiment, and surrender.

I've spent twenty years writing in a professional capacity. Writing proposals, crisis communications, and communications plans for big corporations, and now earning a full-time living as a copywriter, writing coach, and community leader for businesses.

Today I help writers make progress on their passion projects, because even the pros need a guide, and I help creative business owners sound more authentic in their writing.

Because we buy from people we like and trust, we want to write like people we'd like and trust.

The book you're holding in your hands is my third self-published book. The first was a mini-book that I cranked out in three months; the second, *Unfussy Life: An Intuitive Approach to Navigating Change*, took three-and-a-half years — a book that spent half of its gestation time sitting in a folder.

I jumped into writing this book, *Intuitive Writing*, after more than a decade of self-development work and twenty years of writing in a business setting, but only having "writer" attached to my title for the past eight. My challenge to myself was to write it by following all the advice I regularly give my clients and that I'm laying out within its pages.

If you're already scratching your head, well, take a breath and buckle up — we'll get there together, one page at a time.

HOW TO USE THIS BOOK

Use this book to get started. This is the most important thing. Take just one step — today. As your writing coach on this journey, I share lots of tips. These tips aren't going to tell you what to do. That's part of the problem. The authoritarian upbringing many of us received only taught us to look to others for how to act. You're going to learn how to use, and trust, your intuition to write, not sit there while a teacher at the front of the room gives orders.

Start writing on your big or small project right now — as soon as you finish reading this chapter.

Or read the entire book through to the end and then start writing.

Or write as you read the book. Any of these options will work.

You could be a great candidate for getting the words out and revisiting them later. Play with this book as you go. I suggest you read a few pages and then write for twenty-five minutes. And repeat.

You might find that your excitement starts to bubble up as you read. When that happens, save your place in this book, and go write. Ride that wave of inspiration. Trust me. And then, come back to your spot.

I also recommend you keep a notebook nearby at all times. When readers tested this book out, they told me they had tons of new ideas. Make sure you have a place to capture them as you read.

You'll find a lot of lifestyle advice that might not sound so writerly — these are the things that I've found work best to keep my words flowing. I invite you to experiment with these suggestions — try them on and see how they work for you.

There are a lot of ideas in this book. Take as much time as you need, and pause to integrate whenever you like.

Because I'm sure you don't want to read only about me, you'll also find stories from some friends, clients, and writing community members. I've changed the names in some of those stories.

I know a lot of readers treat books like they're precious. This book is anything but. It's a practical field guide, a fun manual. Write in the margins, highlight meaningful pieces, and flag pages for later. If you're an overthinker, resist the urge to try to "read this book right."

And if you're easily overwhelmed, know that this book isn't a to-do list. It's a guide. Overwhelm is a negative state, and you'll want to learn how to write a new story for yourself there too. You'll also read about managing your emotional state.

While writing this book, I followed all the advice I give you in these pages. The result is a piece of work I'm extremely proud of and best of all, there were many pinch-me moments. Planning, writing, and editing this book felt easy. The entire process was joy-filled, aligned, and abundant. And I'd love for writing to feel this way for you too.

Because the idea of intuitive writing is new to a lot of people, you'll find short snippets of advice you can implement right away called **Intuitive Writing Tips**. These are the pages you'll dog-ear. If dog-earing feels savage to you, bust out your sticky notes.

At the end of key chapters, you'll find **Journal Prompts** to help you integrate what you learned. Don't skip these! I know what you're thinking: "I'll go back and do them later."

You won't. I know this because I've said this. Listen, in the information age, we have no shortage of knowledge. What we have though is an implementation problem. These prompts are to support you in slowing down so you can hear what your intuition has to say.

HOW NOT TO USE THIS BOOK

Finish reading this book on writing and decide that you need to read *another* book on writing before you begin . . . writing. That, my friend, is procrastination. And I know that territory all too well because I used to traverse it frequently myself.

Let's be real.

You're reading these words because you're a business owner who needs to create content, you're a pro writer with a passion project that's not getting the attention it deserves, or you have a story to tell and need a cheerleader to tell you that you can do it.

Perhaps your words feel uninspired, disconnected, or like someone else's, leaving you feeling inauthentic.

You probably say you're too busy to write — life and your bread-and-butter work keep getting in the way. Then there are all those fires to put out. You have to do what makes money.

Or maybe you're writing, but every sentence is painful because you overthink every single word.

Whatever your reasons for reading, you're dreaming about writing — and not doing what you deem to be "enough."

I know first-hand how difficult it is to put writing first, especially when it doesn't translate to immediate dollars in your bank account. Writing tends to slip down the list because we've got other shit to do. Money can't be the focus of writing; it's a side effect of being aligned. We'll talk more about this too.

Getting the words out might feel painful, and you want to love the process — really, you do. Maybe you loved it in the past, but that feeling has faded. Well, it's time to take it back.

I used to sit on the train commuting to a corporate job I didn't love, reading books about writing, and dreaming that one day I'd produce volumes of work for my blog, courses, and books.

I was doing everything *except* writing.

Only when I started taking imperfect action did everything change for me.

What you'll discover in these pages is my process. This is what works for me and has worked for lots of my clients and writing community members.

But remember, one of the great things about any process is that it's a way to get started that you can then tweak to make your own. Try on the advice here, do it consistently, and see if you want to change anything to make it work better for you.

MY PROMISE TO YOU, INTUITIVE WRITER

And yes, you totally can call yourself a writer, starting today. Everyone can write — and that includes you.

I'll show you **simple processes** to help you write just about anything — blog posts, website copy, emails, and even a book. You can be in a creative industry, corporate, or work for yourself. It doesn't matter. This advice will help you with whatever you want to write.

You'll have the **enthusiasm** to try new kinds of writing, the **energy** to face the page, and the **confidence** to share your work with others.

Bit by bit, as you share more of your heart, you'll start to **trust yourself** more. And when you trust yourself more, you'll show up for yourself first. And only when you show up for yourself first can you **find joy** in the writing process.

You'll **transform** — from someone who only thinks about writing to someone who is actively, actually, writing — *and* enjoying it.

This is a book about turning off your thinking mind and tuning into your intuition, making writing **accessible and fun** — for people who are stuck in perfectionism and procrastination to those who have written volumes and are finding themselves blocked, and everyone in between.

Let's do this.

THE INTUITIVE WRITER'S PROMISE

I invite you to make this promise to yourself. The best way to work with these statements is to write them down, revising to use language you'd naturally use. Write them in a notebook, then revisit them every time you sit down to write.

I promise . . .

- to put my writing first and write as often and as much as I can — even if some days my brain tries to tell me it's not enough
- to nurture, tend, and heal my body, mind, and spirit
- to fuel my creativity with healthy, whole foods
- to experiment and find what works for me
- to challenge myself to be okay with being uncomfortable
- to stay open to writing what wants to come through
- to commit to myself and my writing practice
- to keep complaints about writing (and everything else) to myself (and eventually stop)
- to trust myself and my intuition
- to send my writing into the world often, and with zero fucks

MY WRITERLY STORY

I'm writing this book while staring out at the water, which has always been my dream. It's not a beachfront ocean property . . . yet, but a neighborhood pond where I get to watch the gators, turtles, and herons swimming and sunning themselves where sunshine is abundant — Florida.

I've moved around *a lot* — fourteen moves in twenty years of marriage, ten of those moves with kids and animals. And the entire time, I've kept writing. There's nothing life can throw my way that will stop me. The distractions certainly slow my writing down at times, leading to dust among the Google Docs, but that's life. We'll also talk about how to handle distractions — because let's face it: they *will* happen.

However, I didn't always lead this expressive, expansive, creative life.

I used to be an expert corporate-ladder climber.

Before launching my copywriting and coaching business, I spent thirteen years working in corporate communications and management consulting for corporations and institutions, including Fortune 500 companies and the US government.

I grew up believing I should get a job at a big company, wear Spanx, work hard, and rack up paychecks and promotions. I thought having an "office job" was the gold standard for success and leading a good life. I learned that following the rules and doing what others told me was the path to getting ahead. And I was really good at it.

As a management consultant, I worked hard, got promotions, and doubled my salary in just a few years. I had also mastered work-life balance before it was cool. I arrived and left the office at reasonable hours, went to the gym at lunch, usually ducked out early on Fridays, and ignored emails on the weekend.

But then, came the layoffs: three in five years.

A year after having my first kid, my managing director called me into his office, where I sat down with some dude from human resources who I'd never met. It took me a minute to realize what was happening. Then I saw the look on my boss's face. I was getting shit-canned — along with many of my coworkers.

I rode the train home from the downtown Chicago office totally numb. "Fuck, I've had a job since I was fifteen — who am I without work?" I asked myself. I managed to hold the tears back until I got home, at which point I crumbled into a soggy mess on the floor. I was a new mom, adding to my stress, not to mention having an upside-down mortgage in 2009 and being a significant financial contributor to the household.

At this time, we'd been toying with the idea of moving from Chicago to Toronto (my motherland) so we could be closer to my family. I'd look for a job in Toronto instead. It happened quickly; I landed a job at BlackBerry in record speed when they were doing exceptionally well – private U2 and Def Leppard concerts kind of well. I landed a fantastic gig as a crisis communications specialist, and they paid to relocate us.

As people swapped their BlackBerrys for iPhones, shares tanked. News trucks flocked outside our buildings a few times a week, so I knew what was coming. This time, I was prepared. When I got called in for my pink slip meeting, I sat down and said, "I know how this works. How much is severance?" — at which point I turned up the volume in the already-awkward room.

Three years after my first layoff, they were rehiring everyone who'd left the consulting company with which I'd gotten my start in Chicago — and they needed us back fast. So my husband and I sold our suburban Toronto home and found ourselves back in Chicago within a month — record-breaking speed for an international move.

This time was different, though. With two young kids, I had little patience for any demands on my time outside of business hours. Soon we lost some contracts (again), and they fired everyone (again). My third layoff.

I discovered the hard way that job security is an illusion — it was time to take a different approach. I had recently started a plant-based food blog, but it was a passion project that didn't pay the bills.

I was also taking a perfectionist corporate approach to it. I published a new blog every single day. This was an act of pretty massive creation because not only was I developing a new recipe every day (on top of my job and parenting two kids under five), I was also writing stories to attach to those recipes, and publishing the whole thing each night.

I wish I could say I did this because I was in the flow. Nope. I created and published every day because I was worried about what people would think. I thought readers wouldn't take me seriously if they came to a food blog with only a few measly posts. Since I was working in the corporate world, I also thought my language needed to be formal so people would take me seriously.

What I didn't realize then (but have since discovered) was that I was *enough.*

I was then, and I am now.

I'm telling you this so you can start adopting this belief about yourself *now*. It'll make not only writing but also sharing your writing much easier.

It wasn't until a few years later (when, incidentally, I had started eating bacon again, only to eventually return to plant-based eating) that I would realize I actually enjoyed writing — and that people were connecting with my personal stories. The ones who were just there for the recipes loved them, too, but I enjoyed the storytelling – and apparently, so did my readers.

After my third layoff, I knew that it was time to create my own job security – and find some damn passion.

By now, I had a growing side business teaching plant-based cooking to clients one-on-one and in group workshops. I thought about taking this side hustle full-time, but it didn't feel like the right move and the financials certainly didn't look like it on paper.

I didn't want to just get "another job." I was so over corporate America. But we were about to close on a house — just five days after that last layoff. I *had* to work. Consulting skills to the rescue! I took another consulting job and got to focus on corporate communications. My new colleagues, a bunch of awesome people, were constantly asking for my writing and editing help — and I loved doing it. I had some freedom to play with more creative writing for the first time and get paid for it.

Fast forward to a performance review two years in, when I told my manager that I wanted to double down on my communication skills. He told me I should focus on being more "well-rounded" instead — meaning I was supposed to learn some stupid tech I had no desire to learn.

I was going to get better at writing whether I had his "approval" or not. I kept with the status quo while quietly doing the work I enjoyed most.

But there was a problem: I was doing so many things . . . and consequently doing a mediocre job. I checked the boxes at my day job, then rushed to get to the next thing. Work, commute, hockey practice, horseback riding, dinner, rinse, and repeat. I was too stressed and scattered to spend more than a minute saying goodnight to my kids.

Something was broken.

Life-work-health balance was what I preached in my lifestyle blog, but I wasn't heeding my own advice. I'd gotten lost somewhere along the way and needed a change — and I needed it urgently.

It was time to create a life and business I was excited about.

I went all-in on writing, specifically, copywriting.

I'd realized what lit me up — writing! I craved more and wanted to do it all the time. I offered to edit all our company's internal communications. They let me, and I loved it. My corporate job gave me a lot of creative freedom, and I learned everything I could about writing. I started building my writer's voice with a key practice that most potential writers overlook . . .

. . . *writing.*

I wanted to help more people with their writing and grow

my business, so I reached out to some of my friends and former colleagues, offering them a few hours of my time to write or edit anything they needed help with — in return for some candid feedback and a testimonial.

A few people took a chance on me, and I was able to give them words they'd been holding in for ages that they could share with the world: A blog post that made editors at glossy magazines pick up the phone. A website that gave a health coach the confidence to quit her job and take her side-hustle full-time. A bio that empowered a photographer to finally share her website. A proposal that inspired potential clients of a budding consultant to say, "Hell yes!" Even a job description that earned a guy a big fat pay raise and promotion at his startup.

I was onto something. I updated my website, archived the recipes, told a few more friends, added a price list, and kept moving forward. I spread the word about my business whenever it came up. Something magical happened — people found me, passed my name along, and hired me. Every evening, I'd write and edit my ass off for my new clients — mainly small business owners and some mid-sized tech businesses.

Clients loved their shiny new words, and they'd pass my name along to someone else, someone else, and someone else. Before I knew it, I had so much extra work in addition to my day job that I started a waiting list.

I explained to the kids that I would be working more than usual for the next few months. I told them it might seem like I was attached to my laptop — and I was. I told them I was doing this extra work now to be around more later. I'd be able to pick them up at the end of the school day and wouldn't need to drop them off at 6:30 a.m. anymore to catch the early train. I'd come on field trips, we could eat breakfast at home instead of in the car, and I'd probably be a heck of a lot happier.

After thirteen years of working for big enterprises, I had read so much corporate business jargon. Worse — I'd had to write a lot of it too. I'd push my corporate clients to write more like humans, and bit by bit, they'd notice a difference. They used to find their own writing boring; now they actually wanted to read what they wrote.

I couldn't write one more word of corporate-speak. It started to hurt physically. By the time I quit my day job, I was sick all the time. My body was screaming at me to make a career change.

I officially hopped off the corporate ladder that was so familiar to me and dove into being my own boss full-time. With the support of my husband and kids, I now get to work wherever I have an internet connection.

Today, writing is my meditation.

I bounce out of bed every morning. Sunday blues are a thing of the past. Daily, I'm inspired by my clients who want to make an impact while being authentic, without feeling fake and salesy.

Along the way, after writing copy on hundreds of clients' websites, blogs, sales pages, and more, I realized that the ones who got the best results were those who were closest to the writing process. They rolled up their sleeves and dug into the words right next to me. They finally started to trust themselves and it showed in their offers. They were the ones who would actually finish their writing, launch new websites, and start booking clients right away.

In 2018, wanting to help more business owners get these results, I started hosting online "writing marathons," in which a dozen or so business owners gathered to write copy. If they got stuck, I'd take a quick peek, and offer feedback to keep them moving. Well, it was a whole lot of fun, and people wrote more copy than they ever had before. Even better — it was damn good copy.

Writing *with* my clients delivers profoundly powerful results. Today, I coach business owners one-on-one and in small groups inside The Intuitive Writing School Community.

Maybe you've already noticed that I do writing and business differently. One difference is that I believe in "good enough." You'll see more polished grammar and sentence structure in my books because I believe all books should see a professional editor. On website copy and blogs, though, good enough will usually do — especially if you're just getting started.

In the current iteration of my career, I've helped hundreds of clients — including tech startups; designers; creatives; naturopathic doctors; and life, health, business, and career coaches — learn to communicate more authentically, write their stories, and stand out in a busy online world.

I believe that the best way to connect is to write. And if you're not writing, you're not connecting — with yourself or with the people who need to hear you.

Intuitive Writing Tip
Your story is yours and yours alone to tell. Telling your story is your right. And, it's a great place to start when embarking on your writing journey.

PART ONE
GETTING STARTED

Before I fully immersed myself in it, I had a lot of wild and misinformed ideas about what the writing life was supposed to look like. You probably do too. In this section, we're going to break down the barriers in the way of you getting started. This might include busting some old stories and, most importantly, navigating through resistance. This is your invitation to suspend everything you've come to believe so you can embrace the intuitive writing life.

CHAPTER 1
NOT WRITING IS MAKING YOU MISERABLE

You probably picked this book up because you're not writing, and it's making you crazy. People who aren't writing and don't care that they aren't writing — this book isn't for them.

Or, on the flip side, you're writing boatloads, but not sharing your gifts with the world. You've turned the faucet on (which is great) and can't seem to stop the flow long enough to edit and publish.

Personally, I have always found writing easy and fun, but a few years ago I found myself not doing the specific writing work I claimed was important to me — in other words, I wasn't working on my creative writing projects.

I was a copywriter who let my first book project sit untouched for a year, collecting Google Doc dust. For months, churning out sentences for my personal writing projects felt painful, slow, and tedious.

Instead of putting my words where I said it was most important to me, I was using up all my creative brainpower to write words for everyone else. I'd dish out ideas to my clients on finishing *their* writing projects, yet I wasn't taking my own advice.

In the summer of 2019, I completely stopped writing just for myself. I felt like I was forcing it, which is a terrible feeling. I also believe that when you're forcing your writing, the reader feels forced to read it. Not good.

I maintained my client work that involved writing but stopped blogging, book writing, and social posting.

I'd had so many starts and stops on my creative projects that I was burnt out thinking about them. I still had a business to run, so I dedicated all my creative energy to writing words for clients.

But here's the thing: Just because I stopped writing for myself didn't mean I stopped *thinking* about writing for myself. On the contrary, I was *obsessing* about that writing. Here I was, right back in my long-train-commute, wishing-I-was-a-writer phase.

This sucked. It wasn't a place I wanted to be. As a copywriter, I met all my deadlines and put my client work first. I'm a recovering people-pleaser and really good at keeping other people happy and putting my own desires last. This is great for running a business — to a point — until it's not anymore.

The message my intuition was shouting at me was:

SURRENDER!

This would become my mantra for the rest of the summer — and, really, my life since then.

Surrendering meant to stop trying to push and force my way to the page. I was going to be okay with not writing. Taking a break was okay — and I could still call myself a writer.

As soon as I adopted this mantra, a weight fell off my shoulders. It was okay. I was okay. And I was still, in fact, enough.

Intuitive Writing Tip
When we're challenged to surrender, it's because we're trying to control something. We have no control. With this knowledge, write with full surrender.

The only reason I can tell you about this now is that I've gotten through to the other side. I'm happy to report that I've spent the last few years writing instead of thinking about writing — and I can retrace the steps for you to follow (and, of course, adapt for yourself).

I also chose to give myself some grace because after we had moved to yet another state (from Illinois to New Jersey) and gotten the kids situated, I had kept up with all my business writing without really taking a breath. And now I really needed one.

The funny thing was, as soon as I decided to pause the blog and put the book edits off until later, I felt the pull to focus on writing email newsletters. Writing an email each week to the people who let me into their inboxes felt light and easy. Writing emails felt personal — and that I could do.

By taking the pressure off from blogging and book writing, I was able to find flow. And instead of continuing to feel shitty about it, in the work I did with my coach (yes, coaches have coaches too), I got really clear on my personal and business values.

After just two months away from the self-created pressure of writing my book, blog posts, and social posts, I found the motivation to write for myself again.

In order to align with my values, in fact, my own writing had to move to the top of my list. My coach and I agreed that I would commit three hours a week to my book projects.

By putting my own writing first, I was telling my brain:

I'm important.

It's safe to be seen.

I show up and serve my clients better when I put myself and my values first.

The work I do matters.

My writing is how I share with the world and create an impact.

There's nothing I have to tell you about writing that's earth-shattering.

It's all very simple:

Put your writing first. And sit down at the page and do your writing. I can't do it for you. Sure, you could pay me to do it for you, but even as one of my copywriting clients, the most powerful and authentic words will come from you.

And yet this requires work and laser focus. For me, it came down to congruence. As a writer who coaches other creatives on how to do their writing, *not* doing my own writing was inauthentic.

To be completely congruent and authentic with myself, I had to put my creativity first. And not just once or some of the time, but all the time. Every day, no matter what demands life threw my way.

This meant pressing pause on consuming — courses, articles, podcasts, and books. No more information input. It meant going to bed on time, so I could wake up ready to go. It also meant looking after myself with movement and good food to have a clear mind when I came to the page.

Here are some of the specific actions I initially took to put my writing first:

- Blocked time on my calendar throughout the week.
- Stayed accountable by tracking my word count, writing, and editing progress.

- Added it to my to-do list each day as the number one task.
- Sent weekly reports of my word count updates to my coach.
- Put my writing work *first* — scheduling a committed meeting with myself every day.

I'd make a plan to write for three hours a week, and sometimes I'd only write for one. I trusted that an hour a week was still progress. It was an hour more than I was doing before. And each week, all I could do was plan to write, carve out the time, sit down, and make it happen. Though the writing was rough, hour by hour, all that time really added up.

When we first get the words out of our brains, the writing isn't usually pretty. It's a whole lot of shitty first draft (SFD) writing, which I'll tell you about in the next section. And that's perfect. So often, we come to the page expecting a final draft to fall out of our fingertips. It doesn't happen that way for me, or for anyone I know.

But what if you're not writing? Maybe you call this "writer's block." You don't know what to write about, starting is too hard, you don't have anything interesting to say, and it's going to take too long.

I call bullshit.

If that blinking cursor taunts you and you just can't seem to get started, I get it because that used to be me. And that feeling is actually always there. Sometimes it's stronger than at other times, though. And it can get quieter, I promise.

When I was at the height of my "block," I'd open up a blank document, all ready to write. I would just sit there, quietly waiting for something prolific and brilliant to fall out of my fingertips. Nothing would happen, so I'd close my laptop, grab my phone, and start to scroll.

The single best way to bust through it is just to write. Write something. Write anything. Write a pile of shit. Write garbage. Expect to write crap. There's no seven-step process, no rules, no secret, no magic pill. And if that's what you were expecting this book to do for you, put it down now.

If it's time to write a blog post and the words aren't coming out, just start. Get it out, no matter how messy it is. Just write something. Anything. Switch gears and write an email, write a letter, write your grocery list, write some intentions for the day, free-write. It will help the words come more easily when you return to that thing you were trying to write in the first place.

Sometimes people come to writing sessions in my writing community and say things like:

"I have no idea what to write today, but I'm just going to start and see what comes up."

Or "I was going to work on my new services copy today, but now that I'm here, I don't feel like it. So I'm going to write something else."

Or "There are eight things I need to write today so I'm going to pick whichever one calls to me first."

Fantastic! I love it when this happens. These smarty-pants blocked the time on their calendar, made a plan, threw out the plan, showed up, and started writing anyway.

In the end, they're still writing — even if it feels slow, clunky, awkward, and not quite right. The only way to bust through writer's block is to go through. Whatever this looks like for you — and it will look different for you each day — is great.

There will always be time for editing, which is a whole other animal. We'll get there. For now, our focus is on getting you writing. Period.

PROCRASTINATION, PERFECTIONISM, & PEOPLE-PLEASING

Back in my corporate days, I'd sit up straight in interviews and confidently announce that my "weakness" was perfectionism. You know, making it sound like my obsession with getting things right was a strength, and that's why they should hire me.

It worked back then, but it doesn't work for me anymore. I was lying to myself and not doing my creative projects any favors.

In a conversation with some business friends one afternoon, I announced, "Oh, I've never really been a perfectionist; I write stuff, sometimes give it a quick review, then publish it."

The next day, I had a tremendous insight — half-assing it *is* a form of perfectionism.

Merriam-Webster defines perfectionism as "a disposition to regard anything short of perfection as unacceptable."

Well, holy shit, that definition sounds fucking exhausting. My personal brand of perfectionism looked like kinda, sorta launching my writing community on my birthday without an actual plan. The built-in safety net: If no one buys, I can chalk it up to not trying that hard.

This kind of action can be fine — but half-assing every launch is not going to be supportive of my long-term business growth.

My form of perfectionism also looks like intentionally choosing low targets that I knew I could hit. If I set a teensy goal, I get to say I did it, and it was a breeze. And even more, I get to keep my "perfect" image up. I avoided failure, when instead, I just needed to reframe failure.

Perfectionism can also show up as keeping all your goals to yourself. If no one knows about them, they'll never know if you missed your target.

This weird habit started for me in grade school. School

came very easily for me. I rarely studied, did my homework the day I got it, listened in class, raised my hand, and did everything I was supposed to do. In return, I brought home tokens of my enough-ness in the form of pats on the back and straight As.

Perfectionism, procrastination, people-pleasing — it's me trying to avoid judgment. It's why I blogged five days a week for the first few months so people would think I was an expert who knew what she was doing. But most importantly, I had to make it look easy. I did that by working so hard I had to force the *je ne sais quoi.* On the surface, I could look like I was "in the flow," but behind the scenes, I was creating my own stress.

Perfectionism for some creative business owners can look like tweaking website copy for months or hiring experts — only to fire them and say they don't understand you. It also looks like waiting to publish a newsletter because you're not sure what to say or spending hours each week obsessing over every email.

I get it. So many of us have our very own brand of perfectionism. Mine was just a little less obvious.

Intuitive Writing Tip

Procrastinating on your writing does not mean you're lazy. Procrastination can often stem from mindset blocks.

You and me, we're no different from each other. I might have more practice pushing through the not-writing part. You can get to the other side. The only difference is a pile of words.

Doing your writing isn't about finding the time, making the time, or creating some new project- or task-management plan. Not writing has to do with procrastination — and that's usually tangled up in perfectionism.

If you're nodding along, then you're likely procrastinating.

In the beginning, as you start writing, you're working to bust through the old story; if you can't take perfect action, you'll take no action. If you can't write a perfect book, blog, or email, you won't do it. You can't take criticism, so you decide to do nothing. It's much safer that way. Well, do you want to be safe, or do you want to have words on the page?

The best way to never get criticized is never to write a thing. And I know that's not why you started reading this book.

If you constantly land in a cycle of procrastination, I want to make it clear that you are not lazy. Far from it. Procrastination can bubble up as a response to wounding. We'll talk about why healing your past wounds is essential to being able to write — and write well. We're all on a lifelong healing journey, and you can absolutely write while healing. I'm doing the healing work right alongside you while I write.

As your writing coach on this journey, my job is to help get you started and keep you going. I'm not here to do the work for you — only you can do that. I'm not here to enable you or listen to your "inner children" listing all of the reasons that you don't have time to, or can't, write. In unhealed people, the inner children are running the show. It's okay for kids to be kids, but kids shouldn't run an adult's life.

I want you to publish your website, your blog, and your books. I want you to write a shitty first draft, quickly edit it, and publish it. I want you to take imperfect action — over and over and over. Over time, your actions (and your writing) will become more aligned.

The world doesn't need your perfect prose.

It needs your words.

It needs you to create the impact that only you can make. Many choose to do nothing. Many choose to overthink all those words and keep them to themselves.

If you're reading this and you've read more than a dozen

books on writing and haven't published your writing yet — I invite you to put this book down for a few minutes and ask yourself if you're procrastinating. Write something super-fast before picking this book back up — take a baby step into the writing habit.

JOURNAL PROMPTS

1. What was your purpose for picking up this book? What do you hope to achieve?
2. What have you tried before?
3. How does perfectionism show up in your writing?
4. What writing are you procrastinating about right now?
5. What will happen if you stop procrastinating? What's possible?

CHAPTER 2
BS-FREE INTUITIVE WRITING ADVICE

Oh, I'm so excited for you. You're about to bust through so many old ideas about writing that no longer serve you. You've probably heard shit-tons of writing advice, maybe tried some, or perhaps forced it to fit.

If this is the first book on writing you've picked up, then yay, you! Hopefully, you've learned by now that the best writing advice is whatever gets you writing.

You'll see some writing advice here that might be the complete opposite of what you've heard before. It goes without saying, but just in case: even if you read these myths I'm about to stick a pin in, and you love these writing practices, and they work for you — you always have permission to do what works for you. Always.

I also invite you to try on some new techniques to see what's effective for you. Just like I tell my kids when they turn their noses up at new foods, "Don't knock it till you try it." Such is true for much of life — except, of course, if you know it's harmful or dark for you — then steer clear.

BS-Free Intuitive Writing Advice #1: Write as often as you like.

If you think that "real" writers write every day, they don't. Some might. I certainly don't. Even during the thirty-day NaNoWriMo challenge (National Novel Writing Month – more on this later), I skipped a day completely, and on another day, all I did was make a list.

There's a lot of bullshit writing advice out there for people to push through when it's not time to push, and when you keep doing that over and over, it can lead to burnout. Push just enough to be uncomfortable, not to the point of pain.

Too many aspiring writers think they need to write daily to call themselves writers. Write every day if you want to.

Intuitive writers write when they motherfucking want to. Period. Fun fact: I used to call my writing community "Write Like a MOFO" before calling it "The Intuitive Writing School Community." I changed it because "MOFO" was getting flagged as sensitive content.

Forcing yourself to write every day because you think you'll lose your writer card if you don't isn't going to do you or your readers any good.

It's like, "Hey reader – I put myself through hell to write this website, email, blog series, ebook, course, novel. I forced myself to write every day, subsisting on white bread and instant coffee. Wanna read it?"

Uh, no, thanks. Putting clean, rested, peaceful energy into your writing is more important than pushing yourself to write when there are truly more pressing things that need your attention.

BS-Free Intuitive Writing Advice #2: Writing is fun and easy.

The idea that all content-creating business owners are handcuffed to their laptops for eighty-hour weeks and all writers are tortured: bullshit.

For myself and most of my clients, even if we don't always honor our bodies, we're learning. And sometimes we skip lunch — but we do show up and do the best we can every day, and that's enough.

Writing is hard when you believe it's hard. It's only difficult because it's new to your unconscious mind. New feels new — and new can feel fun and exciting. You get to choose. If you hold onto the idea that writing sucks and is painful, well, no shit — it'll feel that way.

Any piece of BS writing advice, when we believe it, can turn into a limiting belief that holds us back, and this is one you can choose to rewrite any time you like. Why not do it now?

BS-Free Intuitive Writing Advice #3: Read books you enjoy.

I used to feel embarrassed when seeming intellectuals would talk about classic books — Hemingway, Austen, Brontë. (Honestly, I had to look up some of the classic names and authors for this chapter — and I'm not embarrassed about it). If you love the classics — awesome. If you've never read them, you don't have to.

I used to force myself to read fiction. I saw so many friends racking up reviews and recommendations of novels and wondered what I was missing. I gave novels a solid try, and I just couldn't get into them, so I stopped trying. I prefer reading real stories from real people and learning so I can do better things and be a better human.

Read what you love. Read what inspires you. If you love to write, you probably love to read — and the great reward of reading is you're learning how to write as you do it.

BS-Free Intuitive Writing Advice #4: You can network with anyone you like.

Ever heard the advice that writers should only network with other writers? Well, that's no fun. Variety is the jalapeno pepper of life. In business, do you only want to surround yourself with people doing the same work or in the same industry? That's how we build bubbles. Sometimes a bubble is great, but there's so much to learn when you expand beyond your industry.

Expanding my knowledge outside my industry gives me new ideas and fresh perspectives — more writing inspiration! Among the high-level business masterminds I've been in, the best were those in which the business owners came from different industries. While having some connections in the same field is comforting — to mentor and be mentored — it's great to get real-life and online experiences with a diverse crew to help you feel less lonely and think bigger.

BS-Free Intuitive Writing Advice #5: You can write volumes in slivers of time.

There's no need to retreat to an off-grid cabin in the woods, alone, in order to write. Do you know how many creative projects wouldn't exist if their creators had to disconnect from the world and work alone?

If writing in a remote cabin sounds appealing to you, go for it. I'm telling you this because if the reason you're *not* writing is that you think you need a special secluded environment and a wide-open calendar, then I invite you to explore the cracks of time in your everyday life.

The only time I go to remote cabins in the woods is on vacation, and if I end up writing — cool. Mostly I'm there to unplug from everything, including my writing projects, and get quiet.

Most of my creative work happens at home, a lot of it on the couch or the porch. The rest happens at the hockey rink or horseback riding arenas (while my kids are practicing or taking lessons) or at coffee shops or bars (a great option when coffee shops are busy — you don't have to drink alcohol there either). When I'm writing in a busy public place, I get to keep to myself (introvert perks).

One of my favorite pieces of advice from author Julia Cameron is to write "in the cracks." Just like we don't escape life to hole up somewhere and write, we often don't have six-hour stretches of time to write either. But we do have oodles of shorter chunks. The cracks are the fifteen minutes while you're waiting for your coffee, twenty minutes between meetings, and even five minutes when waiting for water to boil. You'd be amazed at what you could write in just five minutes. Set a timer and go right now — then count your words and prepare to be dazzled.

If you work best with big blocks of time, you can skip the cabin in the woods — but you do need a calendar. Schedule those times now and protect them like a MOFO.

BS-Free Intuitive Writing Advice #6: You can write without ever running into a block.

One of the most common questions I get is this one: "Jacq,

how do I get through this writer's block?"

I respond by asking them to describe what's going on, and they typically say things like this:

I don't know what to write about.

Starting is too hard.

I don't have anything interesting to say.

It's going to take too long.

I'm worried about how I'm going to sell it.

Do any of these statements sound familiar?

To me, these aren't writers' blocks. I used to empathize with writers calling themselves blocked, and now I don't. Because I stopped believing in it.

The question isn't "Am I blocked?", it's "Am I full or empty?"

When you're full, you have plenty of ideas and inspiration. You have to get to the page to let some of it out.

When you're empty, you've completely released all your stories already. The well is dry.

When you feel blocked and can't start, you start blaming others: *Why are they constantly interrupting me? If I didn't have a job or family, I'd have so much focus. If I didn't need to make money or have to cook all this food, I'd have so much energy.*

Or you blame yourself: *I should be better at this. I should know how to do this by now.*

There's a big difference between being blocked and being empty.

When I hear of business owners being blocked, my first question is, "When did you last write?"

Crickets.

Often, they haven't even gotten to the page. They're saying they're blocked when they really haven't done anything except not write while *thinking* about writing. I know this pattern well and can spot it a mile away.

Our inner critic is often so loud and in our faces that it's hard to know when we can put them in their corner. And what helps many stuck writers is having permission to write a piece of shit.

That book on your nightstand, the blog you read on the toilet, the online course you finally just finished, this book — they each started as a Shitty First Draft (SFD). This term, coined by author and writing teacher Anne Lamott, is intended to get writers comfortable with writing crap (note: I didn't say *publishing* crap).

Pretty much everything you've ever seen written anywhere started out as an SFD.

If your writing flows from your fingertips perfectly, error-free, with no pesky dangling modifiers or other grammatical offenses, then you might not be human. *But, if this is you, I'd love to know — maybe you can teach me your ways.*

Writing quickly is a practice of surrendering to the writing process. Writing is an experience, and the more you practice the easier it becomes. Whatever you leave on the page each day is what it is. Your writing practice isn't linear. Surrendering allows for the ebbs and flows.

Most writers, myself included, are intimately familiar with the SFD. When you're aiming for an SFD, writing is easy, fun, and flows like melted chocolate.

Here are some tips for writing a successful SFD:

1. **Turn your brain off and tune into your body.** The SFD isn't for overthinking. Ignore all those red squiggly lines alerting you to typos. To ignore these, I like to blur my eyes, look out the window while I'm typing, and constantly scroll

down so I can't see what I wrote. It can be tempting to go back and start fixing — you'll get to that.

2. **Get it out as quickly as possible.** This is the point. Surrender and simply write. You'll go back and edit later. The stuff you don't edit is the stuff of journals. Setting a timer for twenty-five minutes can help you focus. Like the spicy bean burrito you ate for lunch, it just wants out. Let it out.
3. **Edit later.** When you revisit your SFD — ideally after stepping away for a few minutes, a day, or even a month — you'll have fresh eyeballs and be ready to dive back in and start chiseling out your work of art.
4. **Remember that it's supposed to suck.** As you read your SFD, you might be thinking, "Holy shit, this piece of work is terrible!" Sometimes SFDs never see the light of day or anyone's inbox or the pages of a book. And that's okay. That's the whole point. The SFD is for downloading information onto the page.
5. **Write when you feel like it, even a little bit.** When I get a stroke of inspiration, I'll write a fast and furious SFD and come back to it later. Sometimes "later" means in a few months. When it comes time for me to publish a new blog post or start a big book project, I'll review all my shitty first drafts and see what inspiration I can draw from these nuts and bolts. The gold is in the editing.
6. **It's going to morph.** Sometimes an SFD turns into something entirely different than I had planned. Sometimes it ends up as a PDF download or even a workshop or course. Sometimes it will live

forever as a draft. But at least it's no longer rolling around in my brain.

PROFESSIONAL WRITERS HAVE TROUBLE GETTING STARTED TOO

Meet Lauren, a writing community member who calls herself a writer and found herself utterly blocked.

> I've been a professional writer all of my adult life — copywriter, journalist, advertising, content, all of it. But after some nasty experiences writing for local newspapers, I became utterly blocked: I was unable to write a sentence beyond texting, 'Please bring me a baguette' to my daughter.
>
> I stumbled on The Intuitive Writing School Community through a recommendation in someone's newsletter, and thought this just might be the thing — and I wasn't wrong.
>
> It wasn't immediate. It was a slow change, even frustratingly so, but when I look back at the trail of growth now, I'm pretty amazed. Writing has once again become a source of pleasure; I've found my voice again, and can happily write a blog post and a newsletter on the same day.
>
> I even pulled out some old fiction and have been thinking about dipping back into that. And hey, a book? Why not? Anything is possible with the compassionate support and enthusiasm of Jacq and this group.

I love Lauren's story because what she proved to herself is that by showing up to the page, she's taking action. Only when she chose to show up and give the words an opportunity to come out did she start to find her voice again. Look at the new inspiration that found her – writing fiction! This wasn't even a thought before she joined the community.

Hey, Intuitive Writer. Another BS piece of advice, "Don't share your drafts." Well, I want you to see my very initial – very rough draft of this chapter. Here's an excerpt.

BS writing advice
myth-busting

Oh, I;m so executed for you. You;re about to bust through so many old ideas you have about writing that no longer serve you. You're probably reading this book because youve heard so much writing advice and just dont vibe with it. Or, you;ve been taking all kinds of writing advice and taking it as gospel retain to make it fit your life and it just doesnt work.

If this is the first book on writing you've ever picked up then yay you. Hopefully you;ve learned by now that the best writing advice comes from what works for you. This book is a compilation of what ive seen work for me and my clients. And ecwn then, what works for me and my clients one day doesnt work the next. Thats just how it goes.

It goes without saying, but just in case -- even if you read these myths I'm about to stick a pin in and you love these things – youre always hace the permission to do what works for YOU. Always.

And don't be afraid to try on some new techniques if they dont work for you then you wont know til you try ut. Just like I tell my kids when they tuern their noses up at new foods. Don't knock it til you try it. Such is true for much of life – except of course if you know it's harmful or dark to you or others – then don't do it.

Write every day
If you think that "real" writers write every day, they don't. Some might. Though I certainly don't. Even during NaNoWriMo challenge I skipped a day completely and on another day, all I did was make a list.

Too many aspiring writers think they need to wite every day to call themselves a writer. Write every day if you want to.

Real writers write when they motherfucking want to. Period.

Forciing yourself to wrte because you think you;ll lose your writer card if you don't isn't going to do yourself or your readers any good.

Like , "hey reader – i put myself through hell to write this website, email, blog series, ebook, novel, I forced myself to write every day, wanna read it?"

Uh, no thank you.

Writing is hard
U;kll sum it up to this -- the writing is so hard, and look at me doing it – dont make yourself a victim of words - - that's crap. THe idea that all buiness owners are slaves to their laptops for 80 hour weeks and all writers are tortured -- bullshit.

November 21, 2021

See all those typos? You might think I was drunk when I wrote this. I wasn't. And this is one of my more polished SFDs.

CHAPTER 3
HOW TO GET THROUGH RESISTANCE & START WRITING

You know how it goes. You sit down to write — you have an hour blocked on your calendar and are ready to dive into a project you've been excited about for weeks. Or it's something you know you need to share and perhaps is challenging to write — and now, you finally have the time to get it out, so you prepare your matcha latte, settle into your office chair, and get ready to let the words pour out.

You pop open that blank document and wait. Nothing comes out. You start thinking about how all the pieces fit together, what people will think, what to call it. Your brain is loud.

Ugh — you do not want to write. You want to be anywhere else but here with these words doing this work. You feel a pull inside to push back from your desk, run, and do literally anything other than sitting in front of the blank page. You scroll social media. You do a little "research." Even vacuuming sounds like a good option.

Welcome to resistance.

This chapter is about getting through those first few important and often inevitable minutes of resistance.

I can't think of many business owners or writers who show up to the page with absolutely no resistance. For me, there's always *some* resistance there — even after all these years making writing my business and a creative habit. Especially when I'm not sure what I think about a particular topic yet.

The *only* way through resistance is to jump in and write.

In a session in my writing community, a member asked, "Does the resistance ever go away?"

I paused for a long second. Her great question got me thinking. I had experienced some major resistance back when I decided to stop reading about writing and write instead. It had been a few years since I'd battled with it. Once you get good at something, you stop thinking about it so much.

"No, the resistance is always there," I said. "It just gets less sticky as you practice taking action."

How we get through resistance is the unsexy part — take a small action and write. Build the muscle by repeating the small action over and over again. Short writing sessions, even just twenty minutes at a clip, over time, can produce a massive amount of work.

One of the most common things people say keeps them from writing is not knowing where to start. They're resisting starting because they don't know how.

I truly hope this is the last book you need to read about writing and you'll decide to start. I see so many people taking no action at all because they're in resistance — they think they need to know more before they start writing.

Someone direct messaged me on social media to ask, "How do I get my book out there?"

My first question, "Have you written your book yet?"

You might guess where this is going. Her answer was "no." She hadn't even started writing her book yet. I know this person isn't alone in thinking all the way to the end game of book marketing when they haven't even started writing, let alone planned their book.

Resistance lives in our heads. Our bodies know what to do if we put our brains aside. Imagine removing your brain and putting it in a box beside your desk as you begin writing. Getting through resistance is getting out of your head and into your body. It's the only way.

Resistance is always there in some shape. The resistance you meet today looks different from the resistance you'll meet tomorrow. Sometimes, like fog, it's super dense and it takes a while for the sun to burn it off. Other times it's easy to push through and get to the other side.

I'm so used to taking action now that I don't stop to entertain resistance or pay attention to my brain when it tells me to fold the laundry, check email, or send a text instead of writing. It's like a quick little cloud that passes by — *oh hey, resistance, I see you, and you can keep moving along because I have some writing to do.*

Sometimes resistance is there because of fear, or maybe something deeper. Fear always comes from the reptilian brain. That part of your brain runs from a hungry bear. Getting chased by a bear is less likely these days, depending on where you live, but that part of your brain is still there. It's there for everyone.

There could be fear stemming from something you have to face. You might be thinking back to a crappy grade school teacher or preparing yourself to write about a heavy, controversial, or potentially sensitive topic. You might have fears around what it means to successfully write what you're trying to write. What will it mean? What if people don't like it?

Language is important here too. Instead of saying, "I'm afraid," try saying, "I feel fear about writing this because [insert your reason]." By making the fear something outside of yourself, you're not associating directly with it. You are not the fear. You simply *have* some fear. It's much easier to get rid of something you have than change who you are.

Sometimes resistance comes from something urgent nagging at you. If there's a call you need to make or task you need to attend to before you can write — do that.

Is it possible your resistance is your intuition telling you to avoid something, or are you trying to stay safe — from criticism or crickets? The intuitive writer is able to discern what your inner knowing tells you by taking lots of time, getting quiet, and truly listening.

Intuitive Writing Tip

Resistance may always show up when you write. The goal is to get past those first crucial minutes and start moving your fingers.

There are days to push through resistance, and there are days when pushing won't help at all. Push to the point that lets you know you're getting out of your comfort zone. The more you do, the more natural it will feel over time. Only you know for sure.

As your writing coach, when you tell me you're resisting the page, I'll come back with some questions and nudges and encourage you to get uncomfortable — but I'll never tell you what to do.

Look up what's going on energetically with the planets and the moon or, if you have a menstrual cycle, notice what day you're on (more on all of this later). Is it a time when you naturally need more rest, and you're pushing? You may need to take a break from writing and do some journaling, planning, or reading instead.

From my work and the work of others, I frequently see the biggest resistance comes from the habit of overthinking that keeps your hands tied behind your back.

Expect that your work will change and transform. People often get stuck before they start because they're thinking about the whole process. They're fast-forwarding to the end product — thinking about what the design will look like on their services page, how often they'll write blog posts and newsletters, how they'll design their newsletter banners, pondering book covers, marketing, and distribution before they've even written a word.

And what if your opinion changes?

You're a different person today than you were yesterday, right? What about last year? What about five, ten, twenty years ago?

You're different. So it's only natural to expect that your writing will change too. And that's okay. I look back to some of my old writing and cringe a little — sometimes the language was barfy, and sometimes my beliefs had changed. Those were the things that I wanted and needed to write about at the time. And someone else in the world, also in that snippet of time, needed to read what I had written back then. If you're being called to write something, there's a reason — trust it and get the words out.

You might even have this experience as a reader; perhaps there's an author whose earlier work you enjoyed, but their new work doesn't land with you. That's okay. That author is changing too.

If you have hard things to write that you've been putting off — write those first. I call those energy leaks. That email you've been meaning to send to a client about raising your rates. That response to the volunteer organization that you need to back out of your original promise. Or the message to your last client asking them for a testimonial.

All those things swirling around in your busy brain take up valuable real estate. Now, if those things come up *while* you're writing on your important work — your website, blog, book — keep a notepad nearby and jot those down. Then, come back to the page. This takes training, and the more you repeat this, you'll be training your brain to do it naturally.

Here are some tricks you can try to get past resistance when it creeps up.

1. **Prepare for resistance in the first place.** When I was working on the first draft of this book, I closed all tabs on my browser and only left my book in progress open at the end of the day — so when I opened up my laptop the next morning, the page was there waiting for me. This way, I could start writing immediately, with no room for distraction to sneak in while I navigated to the file. Set yourself up for success as much as possible.
2. **Know resistance is going to happen.** When you expect it to show up, you can greet it and start. You have to start. Once you get moving, the momentum takes over. Step one is getting yourself to the page, step two is writing. So you start.
3. **If you're antsy — move.** Did you move your body at all before you sat down? Get up and try walking, push-ups, squats. Moving your body for

just a few minutes before you start writing will help you focus.

4. **Start your day by emptying your mind with a freewriting or journaling practice** like morning pages (a practice created by Julia Cameron, which you'll see mentioned a lot in this book). When you get the crap out of your busy mind, you can get more quickly to the words you want to write.
5. **Create a writing ritual.** This could be lighting a candle, using an essential oil, sitting in a designated writing spot, or cueing up a certain song or playlist.
6. **Write different things in different spots.** Most of my book writing happens on the couch or patio. If you get a lot of momentum in public places, give coffee shop writing a try. I wrote most of *Unfussy Life* on the couch and edited it at my desk. The couch was for creative work, the desk was for editing and revising.
7. **Play with the Pomodoro technique** — a time management method developed by Francesco Cirillo in the 1980s. The idea is to use a timer to break work into sprints, typically twenty-five minutes, followed by short breaks. The break is a crucial time out from the page — don't skip this step! You can choose to do one cycle a session or play with two or more. If you can write for just twenty-five minutes, then rest and repeat, you'll have done a few things: you showed your brain that you mean business, you took action, and you got some words on the page.

8. **Tune out all media.** If you're choosing to write while reading this book (and I hope you are), keep going. Some writers like to tune out all media while writing while others choose to read and watch things that have nothing to do with their topic.
9. **Wear headphones, earplugs, or whatever you need** to tune out the outside and tune into yourself.
10. **Open up a piece of writing you enjoy** – a book, blog, newsletter – and copy one page of the writing, a word at a time, in a notebook, pen to paper.
11. **Look at an image of your subject matter.** Check out images on DuckDuckGo (at the time of this writing, I prefer this browser over Google for an ad-free, non-curated, and non-tracking experience). Say you're writing about the ocean. Looking at a picture of the beach can unlock fresh ideas and shake things loose in your brain.
12. **At the end of your writing session, leave your last sentence unfinished.** Hemingway suggested stopping in the middle of a sentence in order to easily jump back in. He said, "The best way is always to stop when you are going good and when you know what will happen next. If you do that every day . . . you will never be stuck." By setting the stage for your next writing session, you'll make jumping back into writing much easier.
13. **Write before you do anything else.** Many folks prefer to write first thing in the morning. This way, it's not looming over their heads all day as they go about their business. How can you set up

your day so you can do your writing first thing? When I wrote my first mini-book, I got up every day around 5:00 a.m. because I had a ninety-minute commute to my downtown Chicago office job. If writing didn't happen in those wee hours, it didn't happen at all. I wrote this book in thirty-minute chunks at 8:30 a.m. every day one November.

14. **Explore a new environment.** If getting away from everyday life is essential for your focus, jumpstart a big writing project with a day or two at a nearby hotel or condo rental (or here's that opportunity to try your chops nestled in a log cabin or beachfront condo). I've done out-of-town writing on a few occasions — a small writing retreat with a few close business friends and another time with just one other friend at a hotel an hour away. Seeing how much you can produce when you remove yourself from the day-to-day can give you the boost and confidence you need to keep going. Maybe forty-eight hours of complete immersion is what your writing can use?
15. **Keep yourself accountable with a writing buddy or writing community.** When you're logged into a call or sitting around a table where everyone else is writing, there's nothing else to do but write. And I'm guessing you don't want to be that asshat who's scrolling the web for dinner recipes while everyone else is working on their passion project.
16. **Don't judge the process.** Like the SFD of anything you write — it's messy. Try to think of

writing as operating in the same way as your kitchen faucet. When sitting at the page, it's time to turn the faucet on. When the faucet is on, you have to give the water a place to go. Let the words come to the page. Let them all flow out. Even if, at first, the faucet is full of air and sputtering. Sit still and let the air work its way out, then feel the satisfaction when the water begins to flow. Commit to finishing out the time you said you'd write, and then move on to something else.

17. **Look at your writing to-do list like a menu.** When you're working on a book and you have a list of topics to write on, list them all out like a menu of chapters and choose the chapter you're most energized to write about — or even the one that's easiest for you to start. The same goes for blog posts. You have a dozen ideas to write about — choose the one that stands out or the one that will move the needle most toward a business goal.
18. **Give yourself rewards.** Set your targets — writing for twenty-five minutes, writing three days in a row, writing for thirty days, or hitting a specific word count — then choose rewards that will support and not hinder your goal. Going out and drinking four glasses of wine or eating a big-ass burger dripping with all the fixings and fries will leave you feeling like molasses the next day. Maybe your reward is a massage, a book that's been sitting in your online shopping cart, a new journal, a sweater, or some luxurious socks. When you tie your reward to the effort you put in, every time you look at or use that item, it'll remind you about how

awesome you are and how you met a goal — creating even more feel-good vibes in your brain.

19. **Pick up a pen.** If writing on a computer leaves you feeling drained and exhausted, try writing by hand first. I've worked with many writers who get their ideas out in a notebook first, and then they can edit as they move their writing from the page to the document. Many prefer the speed of typing, but if typing leaves you feeling stuck, choose the easiest option for you.
20. **Talk it out.** Use your voice recorder to skip the blank page and get a lot of words out really fast. This technique works well for external processors — if you get answers when you talk through things with people. If you're an internal processor, you may need to do some quiet meditation on a topic first, then grab your talk-to-text app. The muse often finds us when we're away from our desks, and this is a useful tool if inspiration strikes in the car, while cooking dinner, or out for a walk — or if you've been in front of a computer all day and don't want to look at a screen for one more minute.

These are some strategies that have worked for me. Knowing that one might not work for me every time, having a bank of ideas as a fallback plan is essential.

How you *navigate* resistance will change — it depends on what you're writing, your mood and hormones, and even what's going on with the moon (more on these later).

Remember, if you said this writing work was important to you, show your brain that you mean business and make meaningful progress on it.

When you're feeling resistance, there may be something

deeper to look at. Journaling can help clear the gunk from your head.

JOURNAL PROMPTS

1. Is writing a new thing you're resisting, or is this a pattern for you? What is that pattern – when have you felt this before?
2. Is fear holding you back or keeping you safe? How?
3. What's the best possible outcome of you writing this thing you're resisting?
4. List out all the projects you want to start – give them a place to live to show them you honor them.
5. Finish the sentence: I could start this project if . . .
6. Set the scene: What's your ideal environment, mood, time of day for starting your writing project?
7. Imagine your finished project: What does it look like? How does it feel to hold it in your hands or see it on the screen? What expression do people have on their faces when they see your work? How does your work change this person's life? Can you see the ripple effect?

PART TWO
TENDING MIND, BODY, SOUL

Most people think writing comes entirely from the mind. Intuitive writing incorporates mind, body, spirit, and soul. It's multi-dimensional, physical, and energetic. When you pay attention to all the parts of yourself, you bring a richer experience to the page — and your life. In this section, we'll explore topics you might not associate with writing — like good food, your emotional state, and even some tricks to play on your brain.

CHAPTER 4
MODERN DISTRACTIONS

A good motto for creative living is *garbage in, garbage out*. This includes what I watch, read, listen to, eat, and drink, as well as who I interact with in-person and online.

Especially online. One of the biggest distractions: social media. It can be a fantastic tool for connecting with local communities and business friends. I first met many of the humans I love on social media. Many of my amazing clients came into my life through a referral and then got to know me through social media, and I love using social media to keep in touch with them too.

There's connection . . . and then there's consumption. When I spend more time consuming and scrolling than creating and living, I don't like who I become. It's a procrastination device that keeps me from my focus.

When I started writing *Unfussy Life*, I'd set up little games with myself. Write for thirty minutes, then reward myself with a social media break. Except that "break" would bleed into more than a few minutes, and I'd run out of time to write.

When I realized I was scrolling through pages and pages of

updates without actually even reading anything, I knew something had to give.

If you cannot take a total social media break, you can install apps on your phone and computer to track your social media usage and even remove your social feeds altogether.

Calculate how much time you spend on social media in a day. This might be frightening, and maybe you don't even want to know. Out of curiosity, I once whipped out my calculator to see how much time I'd spend on social media by the time I was one hundred.

To keep the math simple, I estimated spending an hour a day on social media, and if I've been on there since 2007 and spend an hour a day until I'm one hundred, that would mean I'd spent 3.03 years of my life scrolling through the socials.

Three years of looking through pictures of people I don't know, memes, inspiring quotes, magazine-worthy meals, and other people's writing.

Three freaking years is a lot of thumb-flicking. How much could I create in this time if I had the willpower to avoid it altogether?

During the months I was focused on book writing and editing, I took some intentional breaks from social media. Except for checking on my community and private messages once or twice a day, I deleted the apps from my phone, so I could only check from my computer.

Intuitive Writing Tip
Write before you consume any media.

After my last social media break in 2021, I had a revelation that would keep me back on social media for good.

I was chatting with some sisters in a spiritual community

about being on social media. I asked them, "How can you use it knowing it's riddled with darkness?"

The responses surprised me.

"I love social media!"

"Dark? But it's so light-filled!"

"Social media is so fun!"

This was the first time in a long time I'd heard anyone have such a positive relationship with social media. Turned out these ladies knew what they were doing. They only followed light-filled accounts. They look at social media for what it truly is — a distraction if you allow it, but also a tool for sharing our lights and connecting with people who need us most.

By avoiding social media, I was dimming my light. I was staying small — also a function of ego. I returned that day and never looked back. I curated an experience that felt expansive and pushed me to become the next best version of myself by following accounts that inspired me and unfollowing those that didn't.

Now I use social media mainly for business. I no longer scroll endlessly. I post, engage, have conversations, and send some love to the people who show up. When I see accounts I follow promoting bullshit narratives, negativity, and just straight-up darkness — I unfollow. No hard feelings.

JOURNAL PROMPTS

1. What are your go-to distractions?
2. Which platforms do you enjoy most? Why do you enjoy them more than others?
3. The next time you're scrolling, notice your emotions. If something (positive or negative) creeps

up, see how you're feeling and what it was that triggered that.
4. What accounts do you follow that inspire and motivate you?
5. Who do you follow that leaves you feeling tired?
6. How do you feel when you log off?

If social media makes you feel like shit, then quit or take a break. At the very least, curate the hell out of what you let into your precious consciousness.

There are many ways to be mindful of how much you consume.

Create before you consume is one of my favorite practices. If you roll out of bed and the first thing you do is fire up social media, you've already put others' ideas into your mind first before even considering what you think.

Any connection or consumption should feel good. If you sign off from social media feeling angry because you're engaging in a heavy debate with strangers or constantly seeing photos of your friends' latest tropical vacation, and it's leaving you feeling bad about yourself, ask if you really need this feeling and their respective messengers in your life.

Sometimes the comparison game can inspire you to uplevel your own life and push you to try new things. If the game isn't driving you to get out there and do better, you have choices.

If you're following competitors and peers who don't inspire you, put this book down for a minute and go on an unfollowing spree.

Consider just how much time you're spending on social media. Not just for the sake of your sanity and your productivity, but the people around you. I use social media mainly for business and keeping in touch with family and friends, yet there's still a need for balance. How available do you want to be to potential clients, your followers, and readers?

If I was spending three years of my life staring at a screen, that's three years of my kids' lives too. Now that seems completely unfair to them. *Sorry kids, mommy's got years of social media time to log by the time I die* — assuming I live to a ripe old age.

Remember, there's no prize for being the most social on social media.

"BUT I HAVE SO MUCH TO LEARN!"

Learning and reading are important and I dedicate several hours every week to learning. In 2015, I wanted to read more books. When I first discovered the website Goodreads, I was excited — *oh, now I can track how much I'm reading.* Tracking the books I read did this thing where I wanted to read more just to see the book count go up.

That year, I read sixty-seven books — all but two were nonfiction. This was also a year where I was commuting roughly three hours a day, so many were audiobooks.

Initially, my ego was proud of reading all those books. There was a big problem, though. I can't recall a single detail or main lesson from any of them. I was reading too much. Since then, I've intentionally scaled way back on the number of books I read. I choose carefully and no longer feel compelled to finish a book if I'm not into it.

The same goes for guzzling courses, blogs, podcasts, and (obviously) social media.

I was consuming at an alarming rate and missing a key piece. And I wasn't the only one. I see many business owners and aspiring authors missing this too. With a constant and never-ending supply of online courses, workshops, and webinars, we're missing the pause.

We're drinking from the firehose, racing through books, and listening to podcasts and audiobooks at 2x speed.

And for what exactly?

Where's the integration and implementation time?

And, more importantly, *when* will you do your writing?

At first, I resisted the idea of integration — it felt like wasted time. I don't want integration! I want more information! I need more information to be successful.

But more information for what exactly?

More information to consume, so I can forget, not apply a single lesson, and keep moving on?

Integrating information lets it become a part of us, transforming and evolving how we show up, think, act, do our jobs, and live our lives.

It's about the invisible things that we can't measure when we're going a thousand miles per hour without stopping.

We need time to practice and digest what we learn before moving on to the next knowledge acquisition. I decided to stop the mad consumption that was taking me in circles. I intentionally slowed down and savored books. I'd take days in between reading new chapters to integrate the lessons.

Something happened when I took my time learning and implementing as I went — I actually learned. I gave myself time to let ideas sink in and marinate and, therefore, be more effective.

Now, when I take a course, I plan time each week to review materials. And I finish it before signing up for a new one.

The results are the life-proof I was looking for: I do deeper work, have better focus, make steady progress, and grow both personally and in business.

This is also why The Intuitive Writing School Community was born.

It came out of my need to *do* my writing. Because left on my own, I wasn't getting it done. I was doing all the writing for everyone else and had no creativity or energy left for myself.

In my online writing community, we keep the focus on writing and relentless action-taking around our writing. This is why there's only a digestible volume of new content in there each month.

Think about winter — it's nature's time to take a chill pill and snuggle under a weighted blanket. It's where the invisible growth happens. Things are happening beneath the surface that we can't see. The soil is resting, breaking shit down (technical terms here because you know I'm a farmer), and once it's had a rest, spring comes, and seemingly out of nowhere, we see this bright green sprout poking up to say, *Heyyyyy! Look at me! Look at what I made!*

The same goes for information. Except we consume at such an alarming rate, we're leaving undigested bits of food in our crap.

It's like eating a week's worth of meals in one day because they're there. Know what happens when you do that? You'll shit your pants.

Take the twenty-one meals you'd have over a week (or seven if you're all about intermittent fasting) and slow the fuck down.

When you speed up audiobooks, podcasts, and courses, are you retaining any of that information? Are you doing it because they talk too slow? Or are you just trying to finish it? Finish it for what purpose? So you can get to work or get to the next thing?

Author Julia Cameron recommends a media break when

writing — and she suggests pausing all media — no books, blogs, magazines, or anything else.

So, where do we draw the line between staying educated and informed and complete ignorance?

Are you tempted to turn on the TV just to get a glimpse into what's happening in the world?

The more I got to know and honor my empathic nature, the more I noticed how I felt when watching violence on TV. Whether it's the news, a movie, or a TV series, I'd notice my breathing getting shallow and my shoulders creeping up around my ears. If I tried to go to sleep after that, I'd be all wound up and would likely have shitty dreams.

Not to mention that the news, like social media, is designed to keep us glued to the screen out of fear, so we can go live our lives in fear. What, another Covid strain, and this is the worst? I better break out an extra mask and stock up on toilet paper just in case.

Information isn't always power; it can be overwhelming. We need to set up filters and learn to let through only the stuff we need. We get to choose what we take in.

If you've never tried a media diet, try it for just a week. If there's any week to start it, this is the one. Start today, right after reading this, and dedicate the time you would have spent scrolling, watching, reading, or listening and instead focus on the writing you've been putting off. You know, the writing you say you're "too busy" to do.

Here's something to try as you're reading this book: Block additional time after you read — maybe it's ten to thirty minutes right after you've read a few pages in here. Perhaps it's actually doing the journal prompts instead of skimming them and thinking you don't need to. Maybe you'll keep a notebook, sticky notes, a pen, a highlighter, or index cards nearby to capture your insights.

Here are some integration tips to help you digest this book without heartburn (whoa, too much information!) and amnesia (what did I just read?):

- Write morning pages — three full letter-sized pages filled with whatever comes to mind (you'll learn more about these in Chapter 7).
- If you're an external processor, talk out your favorite takeaways into a free transcription app — so you can listen to it later or read your transcribed notes.
- If you take notes while reading, dedicate an hour to go through your notes. Simply review them and notice what comes up.
- Add notes to an online or physical notebook.
- Write a blog post or email newsletter about your lessons.
- Give yourself wide open space to do nothing for at least a day.

When you slow down the rate at which you consume, you may just be delighted to discover that you have a greater capacity for retaining information and maintaining creativity or focus.

CHAPTER 5
LOOKING AFTER YOUR SACRED VESSEL

The famous author wears a cabernet velvet jacket, smokes a cigar, and drinks whiskey as he pens his latest novel in a handsome mahogany bar in Paris.

Sounds so romantic, doesn't it? If you've ever inhaled the smoke of anything stronger than sage or drunk anything more potent than kombucha while writing, however, you know that unless your vessel is clear and cared for, polluting your body won't help you write better, faster, or more brilliantly.

Maybe you've heard the expression "write drunk, edit sober." This sound bite is incorrectly attributed to Hemingway, who did live large and party hard, but reportedly didn't drink while he wrote.

But I do like what this quote is saying, which is that it's a good idea to write from an uninhibited mind. Writing "drunk" to me means to write without ego, your overthinking inner critic, or any outside voice in your head. While some people might say their dance moves improve and their personality gets sparkly after a few mojitos, that's an illusion. You think your ego is being put aside after tossing a few back or puffing on some herbs, but in reality, by using such substances, you're cutting off your flow of consciousness and connection to the Divine.

So, then, how do we write "drunk" and edit with a clear mind?

First, we look after our bodies. If you fuel your body with garbage, you can't expect to produce writing akin to a five-star meal. Looking after my health is my number one value because without it, I have nothing. You wouldn't binge on pizza and beer before going for a run, and you probably wouldn't do the same before writing anything of any importance.

Even though I grew up in a home where we regularly indulged in Diet Coke, Twinkies, and birthday cake — even when there wasn't a birthday on the calendar — I've learned that eating well, resting, and managing my mind allows me to create better work.

Looking after my body first before I sit down to create has only made my practice, business, and actual writing stronger.

Intuitive Writing Tip

What you put into your body will affect your writing. Review what you've put in your body the past week and then compare that to your writing output.

I'm a word doctor, not a body doctor, so the advice I share is what's working for me at the time of writing this book. I've experimented widely with all kinds of practices and I've landed on what works best for me. Play with different practices and routines as you figure out what works best for you.

Here's what my vessel care looks like when I'm focusing on a major personal writing project along with my client work. Let's use a typical weekday during NaNoWriMo as an illustration.

Before I jump in, a word of warning: If you're looking at this list and thinking, *"Holy shit, I couldn't do that every day!"*, please remember that you don't have to. The rest of my life — kids' activities, family dinner — happens while I'm book writing too. Even still, I make sure that every day includes movement, nourishment, hydration, and rest.

6:00–7:00 a.m. Wake up, bathroom, brush teeth, do morning pages, and drink roughly twenty ounces of water. Most days, movement — yoga or weights at the gym.

7:00 a.m. Green juice and/or smoothie, walk the dogs.

8:00 a.m. Shower and get dressed. Ever since I left corporate, I get dressed every day to work at home. Wake the kids for homeschooling (which we started in 2022). Kids make their own breakfasts and direct their schoolwork (after a learning curve).

8:30–9:30 a.m. Daily co-writing, the term I use in my writing community for co-working with a writing focus. I work on my top writing priority of the day while sipping my morning beverage — ceremonial cacao latte with almond milk, mushrooms, maca, and vanilla stevia.

9:30–11:30 a.m. A blend of client work, content writing, editing, and business things.

11:30 a.m. Lunch — something I've batch-cooked on the weekend or leftovers. Almost always, something warm.

12:00–3:00 p.m. More work — meetings, client work, editing, connecting. My calendar is available to the public only during this time.

3:00–4:00 p.m. Client catch-ups, checking messages, and listening to healing and uplifting audios.

4:00–6:00 p.m. Reading, another walk, dinner prep, hanging with the kids. This looks different depending on the day.

6:00–9:00 p.m. Hockey, horseback riding, art, or piano with the kids. Walking, reading, painting, or TV for me — sometimes a combo of these.

9:30–10:30 p.m. In bed to read for a bit and then sleep.

This might look either boring or overwhelming to you, but there's a rhythm in the sameness and soundtrack of each day that works for me. I work weekends when I'm inspired. Throw in a kid's hockey tournament or some travel, and there's little to no writing happening. My weekends are full of family experiences, so I do most writing and editing on weekdays.

When writing this book, I committed to writing with my community for thirty minutes a day, every day. This was fine Monday through Friday but since I normally don't write on weekends, my energy was *drained*. Since I'd made a commitment to lead the community on weekends, though, I showed up and wrote what I could during that time, and then logged off. Next time, I'll protect the weekend hours to go with the flow and only write if I want to.

FOOD IS WRITING FUEL

Here's the foundation of my diet and why I believe it matters. I mainly eat plants. I know food is a triggery topic. There's a lot of cultural conditioning around what we put in our mouths. I'm not going to tell you what to do, only share what works based on my experience.

Looking after your basic needs (like food) gives you more time and better focus for your important writing projects.

We know that energy is everything. What you eat is energy, and it transmutes into energy for your body. This means I eat as many foods as possible each day that have a high vibration. Eating "dead" foods — meat and anything heavily processed — carries fear and low vibes. By eating high-frequency foods —

smoothies, green juices, bright veggies, nuts, seeds, legumes – I feel good in my body. And when I feel clear, I can write well. No brain fog, sugar crashes, or naps required.

My diet is primarily whole food and plant-based, which means yes to fruits, vegetables, grains, nuts, seeds, and legumes, and no to dairy, animals, and gluten.

And I buy organic, non-GMO, sustainably farmed veggies and fruits as much as possible.

If it has an ingredient list, it's not a whole food, so I eat these sparingly. I'll still enjoy french fries, chips and guac, and potato chips a few times a month.

If you want to experiment, there's no shortage of cookbooks out there to help you eat energy-supporting foods from the earth. Find some of my favorites in the resources.

BATCH-COOKING BASICS

Now I'm going to give you a little kitchen lesson. I know you may be thinking, *This is supposed to be a book on writing – why are you talking about cooking?*

Because it matters. Remember, we're considering the Intuitive Writer as a whole person, not just who you are when your fingers are on a keyboard. If you eat well and take the time to plan and prep your food for the week, it makes everything else easier. You'll be looked after and cared for so you can bring your whole brilliant self to your words. Batch cooking is like batch writing (which we'll also talk about). It's cooking more food, fewer times a week. It's perfect for writers because there's no wasted time and energy thinking about what you should make for dinner or spending hours getting lost online scouring for recipes. Before starting my copywriting business, I taught batch-cooking workshops to busy people.

Here are some reasons why cooking once a week rocks:

- Clean bulky things like the food processor just once a week
- No roasting pans to wash midweek
- There are few pots and pans to wash; only use them to make pasta or reheat during the week
- Less clean-up during the week — the cutting board is cleaner, knives stay clean
- Leftovers are easily assembled for healthy fast-food lunches
- Easy to customize all meals to each family member's tastes or needs
- The oven is only used once a week, saving energy
- Less cooking splatters on your clothes, meaning less laundry
- Opening the refrigerator to a bunch of ready-to-go, nourishing options feels beyond abundant and comforting to your creative soul

The prep and cook event usually takes an hour and a half to two hours. When I'm done and have a fridge full of ready-to-eat food, the satisfaction is huge! So is wandering into the kitchen, starving after a focused writing session, and being able to assemble or heat up a satisfying meal in a few minutes. It's a life-changer that sets me up for an afternoon of writing success.

How I save five hours a week.

If you make dinner at home five nights a week, investing twenty minutes in planning ahead can save you at least five hours a week. Meal planning takes a few minutes of thought and a little time in the kitchen. The results are well worth it, saving you time, money, and energy — all of which you can put toward your creative projects.

Meal inspiration starts with fresh produce.

Survey the fridge and pantry for items you need to use or restock. Break out your cookbooks to pick your dinners for the week and make a list. I put together a loose plan for dinners, and the rest falls into place. Read on for some simple, plant-based meal inspiration. I start with what's local and fresh to drive what I eat, which usually means, for example, no strawberry salads with delicate greens in January in the northern hemisphere.

Shop once a week for food.

You may run out of things here and there throughout the week. If you have grocery delivery, get what you can get delivered to your door, saving you even more time at the grocery store. You'll also save money (yay, more books!) from buying what you need instead of stocking up on a bunch of shit you don't.

Prep on weekends.

It's even better if you can schedule your food prep time before house cleaning. This is where the fun begins. When you get home from the store, crank some tunes or an audiobook, and get to work. Below are the steps I follow.

Prep:

- Wash and dry leafy greens and herbs and let air dry while doing everything else. Prep what you'll use in your recipes, then wrap the rest in towels

- Peel carrots, chop or shred them to throw into salads, stir-fries, sauces, juices, or smoothies
- Freeze bananas (peel, break into chunks, put into a baggie, and freeze) for smoothies
- Leave the following alone until you're ready to use: beets, onions, tomatoes, fruit

Cook and store:

- Roast chopped carrots, broccoli, cauliflower, squash, potatoes, or root veggies
- Rice and/or quinoa: cook a big batch for the week (two to three cups dry) — use for curries, rice bowls, soup, burritos, salads
- Soup: make a big batch of soup; squash, sweet potato, or tomato soup are easy and keep well in the fridge
- Dips: make hummus or another bean dip
- Sauces: make tomato sauce, pesto, salad dressing

Once these cooked and ready-to-go foods are in your fridge, your kitchen becomes a healthy fast-food restaurant. Mix and match all your prepped items — hummus goes on pasta or potatoes with wilted greens, as a snack for chopped veggies, or in a sandwich or wrap. Rice can be a base for a quick stir fry or stirred into soups to make them more filling.

MY SIMPLE MEAL PLAN DURING BOOK-WRITING SEASON

Breakfast

A green smoothie a day keeps writer's block away. I make a smoothie fresh each morning.

- Collard greens, blueberries, banana, chia, cinnamon, plant milk, chocolate protein
- Spinach, broccoli stems, banana, apple, plant milk, hemp seeds, vanilla protein
- Romaine, pear, parsley, ginger, flax seed, coconut water
- Chard, ginger, apple, vanilla protein, lemon, plant milk
- Kale, cherries, banana, beets, flax, chocolate protein

Dinner

I list dinner before lunch because I plan our dinners and cook more than I need. This ensures I always have a warm, healthy lunch.

- Butternut squash and red potato curry over rice
- Mushroom and tomato sauce over gluten-free pasta
- Quinoa, beans, hummus, sunflower or pumpkin seeds, avocado, pesto
- Veggie burgers with salad and baked sweet potatoes
- Taco salad with beans, greens, tomato, avocado, cilantro, lime, peppers, onions
- Portobellos with roasted carrots and mashed potatoes

Lunch

Leftovers rule around here. Improvise leftovers from dinner to mix and match for lunch.

- Curried squash over salad
- Kale, pesto, chickpea, hemp seed salad
- Salad with shredded carrots, beets, walnuts, avocado
- Black bean and rice soup
- Veggie burgers, avocado, and tomato over mixed greens
- Portobellos in lettuce or collard wraps
- Roasted cauliflower or broccoli soup

Before your next writing project, explore your well-being routine and see what needs an upgrade. Your body of work will thank you.

CHAPTER 6
LOOKING AFTER YOUR EMOTIONS & SOUL

We're whole beings. Humans are complex, beautiful, emotional creatures. When we look after our body, mind, and soul, it sets us up for success in other areas of our lives. And here, we're focused on writing success. In my corporate ladder climbing days, I didn't think much about eating well. I certainly didn't think about managing my emotional state. I pushed, forced, and muscled my way through to results. Sure, you could say it worked, but I wasn't thriving.

It wasn't until I started nurturing all the parts of me that writing started to feel easier. My writing naturally connected with people. When I put my entire vessel first, I can come to the page clear, calm, and focused. Looking after my emotions and soul are what I call invisible work. When I sweat on the stair climber a dozen times a month, others can see the results. Getting quiet, mediating, and grounding — others might detect a change. This is when people say, "Something's different about you but I can't quite put my finger on it." *It's the soul work I've been doing.*

Here are some practical suggestions to nurture all those invisible things.

GET QUIET

Spending some time every day in silence is essential, even if it's just five minutes. If I don't get quiet and listen to my thoughts and use this time to talk to God, Jesus, and my higher self, I'll only be regurgitating everyone else's ideas. What I'll be calling my intuition is actually everyone else's voices I hear in my head.

I get how hard sitting quietly can be. It took me years to find what works for me, and I still often get interrupted the second I close my eyes.

Closing your eyes and taking deep breaths has some positive benefits. Notably, getting in touch with your inner self, keeping calm, helping manage your emotional state, and deepening your breathing will increase your mental focus and make you more fun to be around. It's also been proven to lower blood pressure and soothe the nervous system.

Tuning in can be easy, and you can work it into your day.

I especially love that half-awake state first thing in the morning before my brain is all the way online and running to-do lists. I lie in bed, completely still, scanning my body for any sensations, feeling a deep appreciation for anything — *I love these bedsheets. This breeze from the window feels so good.*

From this place, I might ask questions I'm pondering and tune into my body for answers. Before the day has had a chance to tell me what to think, I listen to myself — literally the most important thing and the only thing that matters.

Small, mindful moments add up over time. If I'm paying attention and being present, all those moments accumulate into a happier life. And it's so much easier to pay attention to the kids and give them my undivided attention instead of simultaneously listening to them, making dinner, and thinking about the writing I need to do.

In the shower, I take my time, feel the water, and enjoy the shower — instead of mentally reviewing my calendar and forgetting to rinse out the conditioner.

When washing dishes, I just wash the dishes. Pay attention to those tiny pockets during your daily routines where you can deliberately invest your time to practice getting quiet and listening.

GROUND

Grounding, also called earthing, is tuning into the energy that we get naturally from the earth. There's not a ton of research on this topic yet, but if you've ever felt recharged by nestling your feet in the sand, then you might enjoy this.

Some say that putting our bodies in direct contact with the earth can help us feel calmer, more centered, and more relaxed. Most days at lunch, I sit outside, enjoy my home-cooked meal in the sun, and watch my dogs roll around in the grass. They don't have a care in the world. They're busy soaking up that earth energy.

If you live where it's cold as fuck for six months out of the year, you can put your feet in the snow. I sometimes did this for a minute or two each morning when I lived in the northern tundra. Be mindful of frostbite.

Simply petting your cat or dog, being around plants, and eating more fresh foods from the earth — especially green ones — can restore our sense of peace. When we're cool as a cucumber and centered, we can more easily hear our intuition.

MEDITATE

I meditate for a few minutes most days too. We seem to think that meditation has to be this big two-hour event to be effective.

Even if you do it for three minutes and don't post it on social media later, it still happened.

The more we get out of our heads and into where we are at a given moment, the more we create conscious change and people will start to notice a shift in our general level of awesomeness.

I enjoy a few deep breaths every time I sit down at my desk — finding stillness and feeling grounded before I even lay my fingers on the keyboard to help the words flow (even if they're utter garbage sometimes).

Writing itself can also be meditation. Because I come to the page grounded and tuned in, writing feels nurturing. While I'm writing, I make sure to stop and pay attention to my breath. Am I breathing while I'm writing? Feeling my butt on the seat? Is my focus completely on the words in front of me? Occasionally I'll close my eyes to figure out what I want to say next if I get stuck in between sentences.

While it might be easy to skip these seemingly "extra" things in the name of better writing, I encourage you to give them a try. I think that the book you're reading now feels good to read because I've invested (and will continue to invest) in becoming a master of my energy. You're consuming the work of someone who thinks not just about the words, but *how* they arrive onto the page. Investing in the invisible work is an investment in your writing.

JOURNAL PROMPTS

1. Think back to the last time you enjoyed writing something. What were you writing?
2. What other (non-writing) activities do you find calm in?

3. Make a note to linger in bed tomorrow and notice how you're feeling. Then, grab a notebook and freewrite for as long as you like.

CHAPTER 7
MORNING PAGES

When clients bring me a writing problem or frustration, almost every time I ask them, "Are you doing your morning pages?" I'm sure they're sick of me asking this. But it really is effective for so many things.

When you feel stretched too thin, you're all up in your brain, and you think you're too busy to take a breath, it means you need to slow down and listen. When you're feeling overly busy and overwhelmed, stopping and writing might be the last thing you want to do — especially with pen and paper.

But slowing down and getting out of your head and back into your body is essential, especially when you feel buried in work, meetings, clients, deliverables, family, obligations, and responsibilities.

When I'm feeling this way, it usually means I've gotten out of touch — out of touch with myself. Morning pages are one of my most reliable tools for getting back in touch.

Morning pages are described in Julia Cameron's book *The Artist's Way,* and you've seen me mention them several times already.

They're simply three full letter-sized pages of what I like to call "word vomit" — whatever comes out of your brain first thing in the morning — written longhand, with no editing, and definitely no filter.

I first discovered them in 2015 and got myself into a daily habit of writing every morning with my coffee. And then, between moves, life, school, and routine changes, this daily writing practice was the first to go.

Today, I give myself the grace to write them at some point in the morning. While the goddess of morning pages recommends writing them first before you do anything else, that doesn't always work for me. When I want to be mindful of everyone else sleeping, I sit on the bathroom floor and write them. Unsexy, but it gets the job done. When I'm eyeballs-deep in a big creative project, the idea of staying still to write three pages can feel daunting — so sometimes I might skip them. Or I may write for just five minutes and give myself a pass on the three-page goal.

But whenever I skip them, I regret it.

For the months I was working on this book, I committed to daily morning pages and found that the writing I did later in the day came more easily.

Stream-of-consciousness writing is a powerful tool to clear the cobwebs away and clarify what I'm going to write. Morning pages are a great access point for this. And you can adapt them slightly in the ways described above, or do them the way Cameron originally designed them. In any case, there are many situations in which they can come in handy.

I prescribe morning pages:

- When you feel overwhelmed, angry, scared, tired, bored, happy, sad, excited, abundant — basically, all the time

- When you're writing something difficult that you need to process and crave a safe space
- When you're doing inner work or healing wounds, and events and emotions are bubbling up to the surface — which is life work, so again, *all the time*
- When something happens, and you're not sure what to think about it
- To get the junk out of the corners of your busy brain
- For jumping out of your head and into your body with a pen-to-paper practice
- When you need to refill your creative well — if it runneth dry, these pages can fill that shit up
- When you need help to move past creative blocks
- When you just want to get the crap out of your head and get on with your day

HOW TO GET STARTED

If you haven't started writing morning pages yet — and especially if you're not writing the stuff you say you're going to write — start now. There's no need to procrastinate further and wait until you've read *The Artist's Way*. Just grab a letter-sized notebook (the ones from the school supplies section will do) and write quickly on three full pages, no abbreviating.

Don't obsess over which notebook to use. I've bought plain ones in bulk, fancy unlined ones with hardcovers, and even luxurious sketchbook-sized ones. The key is to pick one and get started. Overthinking your notebook and pen is procrastination.

Write whatever pops into your mind — *yes, even the weird shit that pops in.* If you're worried about someone reading it and thinking you're riding the crazy train, that's a sign that you're doing it right.

And remember, there's no wrong way to write morning pages. With kids, sports, and life, some days it just doesn't happen, or you write one page. High-five yourself and move on. Write more later, or do it tomorrow. The goal is only to write — three pages.

Whine and complain, let it all out, and then move on. In Chapter 9, you'll read my feel-good spin on how to wrap it up.

Write morning pages and then put them away. There's no need to revisit them. Write fast, surrender to the process, and move on. They're for your eyes only.

Create a daily habit. Set your notebook out by your latte cup, on your nightstand, or front and center on your desk, and take just fifteen minutes. If you don't see a big difference in your clarity, creativity, and mental energy in three months, move on. If you miss a day and miss writing them, go back to the practice.

When you finish a notebook, recycle or burn the pages (perhaps during a full moon — a great time to release what you no longer need). I can think of no good reason to keep that energy around.

Meet Olga, a former client of mine, who found tremendous healing in journaling during a truly terrifying time. Here's her story.

> I cried for eight consecutive months.
>
> What does a nineteen-year-old refugee do to find comfort, connection, and healing in a place that feels so cold and distant from home? At a time when there were no FaceTime, Zoom, Instagram, or iPhones?
>
> Having my once expansive world reduced to the four walls of a tiny bedroom with four beds for

each of my family members in a shelter for refugees was shocking, to say the least.

My entry into North America was not "in search of the dream" like many immigrants; rather, it was forced, and I had to leave the dream behind without notice. My life in Colombia was a dream just before my father was kidnapped and a terrorist group persecuted us with no mercy.

Secluded in a small bedroom, with five people living in it, all of us grieving our own losses, I began what was going to be an eight-month marathon of tears.

When I left my homeland, I had nothing with me — nothing. As soon as we arrived at the refugee shelter miles and oceans away from home, I was gifted a black spiral notebook.

I didn't know it then, but that dollar store notebook became my place to heal.

Every morning, as soon as I would wake up alongside the heaviness of my heart, I had instant tears. My soul was sad. I had left everything behind. My grandparents, our dog, my friends, my boyfriend, my university, my house, my country, my culture, and my life as I knew it. All of that combined felt like a heavy brick on my chest, bringing me to nonstop tears.

My mom would suffer from seeing me so sad. Not only did she have to cope with her own grief, but she also had to witness her children's grief. Particularly mine, which seemed stronger than my siblings'.

Aware that my tears and sadness would affect

my mom, I intuitively decided to go into the bathroom with my notebook whenever I had strong emotions.

Sitting in the mud with my emotions and journal, I wrote pages upon pages. I let that notebook and many others witness all my emotions. It took eight months.

Journaling every day was the only help I received and, if I'm perfectly honest, the only help I needed.

Journaling connected me to myself. And in a beautiful, judgment-free way, journaling allowed me to process, express, and turn the page. Literally and emotionally.

I wrote my way to healing.

As the months passed, journaling became a source of meditation and a place to find my inner wisdom.

I started noticing a trend. Each journaling entry began to end with steps for the next day based on my daily awareness. I didn't know it then, but this was the start of my work as a life coach.

My very first client: myself.

If it hadn't been for my notebook and journaling sessions, the trauma I experienced at a time when my brain wasn't even fully developed could have had detrimental consequences to my mental health.

But instead, this traumatic experience left me with a profound lesson: journaling heals broken hearts.

Whatever you're navigating, you'll find strength when you come to the page.

CHAPTER 8

MANAGING YOUR STATE

I learned all about state management from the Neuro-Linguistic Programming (NLP) master coach and trainer I've worked with for years. The breakthrough work I did with her changed everything for me.

NLP operates through the intentional use of language to bring about changes in our thoughts and behavior. We know our thoughts are powerful. NLP studies the effects of language on our actions. And our actions drive our results.

A significant component of NLP is about learning how to control your state deliberately — knowing that a state is a condition or way of being, as concerning circumstances or a mental or emotional condition. Your state is how you *feel.*

When you're sitting at the page feeling fear, anxiety, anger, or doubt, these are all negative emotions. And they can be a bitch. The problem with these emotions is that we, as conditioned humans, have a negativity bias — our brain is wired to notice and feel negative things more than positive ones. And it takes work to get into, and stay in, a more positive state.

WHY WE WANT TO BE IN A POSITIVE STATE WHEN WE'RE WRITING

A negative state feels like shit. When we associate feeling shitty with an activity, we'll want to do everything we can to avoid it. If writing doesn't feel good, we won't want to write. That's how drafts of book chapters collect dust.

On the other hand, if you feel really great when writing, you'll want to write, and that vibe will come across in your words. *Your energy matters.* And when you put good vibes into your work, your readers will pick up on that. Therefore, writing with clear energy is a win-win for everyone.

HOW TO TRAIN YOUR STATE

The good news is that you can manage your state ahead of time and ensure more writing days happen from a clear, calm, and grounded state.

To train your state, you'll train your unconscious mind.

Part of the work I did with my NLP coach was intentionally focusing on what I wanted, taking deliberate action, and doing regular hypnosis to stay relaxed because a relaxed mind is calmer and more creative — and that's what we want as intuitive writers.

Another piece is paying close attention to my current state and intentionally making shifts whenever I feel myself about to go down a shit spiral.

Sure, I have my days. Some weeks I'm just on a roll, feeling fantastic, productive, and full of creative ideas. And then I hit a slump.

It always happens when I get busy. Too busy to do the work I say I want to do and too busy to make things happen. Too busy to eat well — when I notice I'm reaching for junk food (what very little I keep in the house).

When I get this way, I feel overwhelmed (which is a negative state). And when I'm overwhelmed, there's no time for movement, meditation, or salad, and my mind is anything but relaxed — only making the problem (and my writing) worse. By the time I notice these patterns, I realize that the feelings of overwhelm have been there for a while.

Unless you can kick a negative state's ass quickly, that negative state is only going to amplify. That's because your unconscious mind takes the essence of your focus and creates more of it.

When you're overwhelmed, you're sending this message to your unconscious mind: "Let's find more overwhelm!"

So, when I notice that one area of my life is feeling dull, I can likely notice some listless feelings and less-than-ideal behavior in other areas. If I'm not looking after my health, I'm probably ignoring my relationships and watching shitty television instead of reading books that will nourish my mind.

I noticed (and confirmed the science with my coach) that if I focus on one area, another area improves. If you're focused on improving your writing and your relationship to writing (hence, reading this book), you'll probably notice that other areas of your life are expanding in beautiful ways too.

When you learn how to manage your state, you're going to be able to manage your outcomes. When you're relaxed, focused, and in control, what you create will look different from what you create if you're in a negative state. So if your desired outcome is killer copy on your website, a growing body of work on your blog, or a book that you're proud to show off — start with your state and work backward.

Here are some suggestions for keeping your state in check:

- **Notice it.** Start by simply paying attention to what you're feeling. No need to judge it as good or bad — just pay attention and get curious about why you feel the way you do.
- First thing in the morning, focus on getting into a **positive state**. Then continue to consciously shift your state a few times throughout the day and again before you go to bed.
- **Morning pages** are a great spot to work out the details or find the root cause of your state. When you notice you're writing about a shitty state for days, you might see where you're avoiding action. Also, know that living in a shitty state for days is a recipe for disaster, completely unnecessary, and detrimental. You always have the power to interrupt a negative state.
- If you **notice a negative state, take action quickly**. The key is to take immediate action to change your state — first to a more neutral one, then to a positive one. The sooner you catch a negative state, the better. It's a lot harder to stop a speeding freight train. To do this, try imagining a giant red X over the thought, thinking, *reject, delete, cancel,* and then watch it disintegrate.
- When you're in a negative state, do some **quick reverse engineering** to figure out how you got there and plan only a short visit. Go back to the last time you remember feeling good and notice what happened afterward. By the time you notice the negative state, chances are you've been pushing against something for a while.

- Begin to reframe and **direct your energy toward the next best thing** you *could* feel. If you're feeling crappy from a rejection letter or because a prospective client said no to working with you, shifting to feeling joy might be too big of a leap. Instead, see if you can get to a state of comfort or relaxation. Try anything that can bring relief, from music to a walk — anything to interrupt the state before it creates momentum. Once you're in a slightly more positive state, investigate what would be the next best thing you could feel. And go from there.

The key is to manage your state proactively. When you get quiet and listen to what your body wants to tell you, you can make tiny tweaks to get into a better-feeling place. Gradually you'll find yourself feeling more peaceful. Suddenly you'll notice you're seeing more desirable results.

JOURNAL PROMPTS

The more often you get into a positive state, the easier it is to stay there. Feeling good frees up energy and allows you to access your internal power. Negative emotions literally weigh down your nervous system. Positive emotions are lighter by nature — that's why intentionally getting into a positive state is a more fruitful long-term strategy than cleaning up a negative state once you're already in it. Here are a few writing prompts to help you get yourself into a positive state:

1. When was the last time you felt terrific?
2. What were you doing the last time you were having fun?

3. Bring your favorite comedy movie to mind — see if you can find a quick clip or movie trailer online. Watch it, then write about what you love about it.

CHAPTER 9
PLANTING SEEDS IN YOUR UNCONSCIOUS MIND

You're reading this book because you've got some writing goals – whether they're big or small, they're uniquely yours and only yours. Get your unconscious mind on board first to make achieving these goals easier.

Every word in this book is included intentionally because the language you use in your mind is just as significant as the language you're reading in these pages.

It's important to know that when it comes to getting a boost from your unconscious mind to make changes in your life, it's smart to make incremental goals.

Let me back up and tell you what your unconscious mind is.

You might know the unconscious mind as the "subconscious" mind. The way I learned NLP was to say "unconscious" mind because "sub" implies substitute, subpar, or subordinate. And since NLP is entirely focused on language (I mean, language is literally NLP's middle name), we use words intentionally. Our unconscious minds are powerful MOFOs that we can use to support our writing goals (and really, our entire lives).

Your unconscious mind is what's controlling your breathing, blinking, and heart beating. You don't have to force these things to happen; they happen because the unconscious mind is doing its job. You also don't need to tell your unconscious mind to "do better" at breathing — it has the wisdom required to do so and it doesn't need your help.

It's also your best friend and ally when it comes to helping you with your writing goals. It's the friend you can count on to help you with your stickiest sentence structure problem or the headline for an article you've been thinking about for an hour.

I like to think of my unconscious mind as my favorite assistant. It works *for* me, and if I keep it healthy, train it, feed it properly, and look after it, it'll look after me.

Like an assistant, this part of your brain needs clear instructions. In fact, you've been (unwittingly) sending instructions to your unconscious mind your entire life. The only issue is that the instructions have most likely been unconscious. However, the good news is, you have the power to train your unconscious mind *consciously*. Cool shit, right?

Making intentional changes to how you write and edit can be challenging. But now that you're about a third of the way through this book, you're taking more action than most of the population. Seriously, most people only *think* about writing. By reading these pages, your unconscious mind is getting buckled in and ready for the ride. You've totally got this — so keep going!

We need all the support we can get to create lasting change in our lives. And since our unconscious mind delivers our reality, it must be fully on board with the shifts we want to make.

This book introduces a series of changes to your writing and editing process that may be entirely new for you. It's going to require conscious effort to try on these new strategies. And it'll take time before it starts to feel effortless.

Many writers try a new method for a few days, fall off the wagon, and then think, "That's a stupid strategy; it doesn't work for me."

This is the case when it comes to all areas of our life and with writing. Writing is simply easier to measure. We have writing goals such as word count, consistency, publishing schedules, and article and newsletter timelines.

Say you set a writing goal that you've previously (and unintentionally) programmed your unconscious mind to believe is unattainable — it exceeds your current programming because you've created beliefs about what you *can* do. Linguistically speaking, this is significantly different from what you *can't* do.

Anything we haven't done before will be outside what the conscious mind knows we can do. But you can make the leap by breaking down a big goal into smaller goals, making it easier for your unconscious mind to get on board. The key is *always* to take action. Behavior trains the brain and focuses energy in the direction of the behavior. Getting your unconscious mind on board with your goals is the key to making it feel so much easier.

Imagine you're writing your first memoir. You've never done it before, so your brain and body might feel a little lost. Before starting your book project, the only things you wrote previously were some emails and a handful of social posts.

Now, to get to the volume of writing required for a book, that's a giant leap. And since you haven't come close to writing anything more than a few hundred words long, your unconscious mind doesn't believe you can do it and doesn't have the hardwiring (neurology) to support you — yet.

So what's an aspiring author like you supposed to do? Commit to a life of social captions with daily character limits that are irrelevant after twenty minutes?

Not at all. Well, you can do that, but I'm guessing you

picked up this book because you have other plans. Keep letting those big dreams inspire you and keep making those beautiful writing goals.

Here, I'll share how my NLP breakthrough coach helped me finish my last book. Hopefully this will inspire you to start playing with your writing goals in a new way – one that could be your ticket to writing like your baddest, most intuitive self.

1. Create a solid foundation for hitting your writing goals.

If you've been focused on writing your memoir (swap this example out for what you want to write) and haven't done it yet, your unconscious mind simply isn't on board yet. Your unconscious mind is running a competing program that doesn't include writing a memoir yet.

So for every "I don't," there's an "I do." So you don't write (yet) because your unconscious mind hasn't made writing a priority. But the more you *do* write, the more writing will become a priority.

To achieve your writing goals, build solid ground for success so that you can begin to see some wins from your efforts. So let go of any limiting beliefs, especially around what kind of business owner, creator, or writer you are, as these beliefs might be unconsciously keeping you from being the successful rock star you could be.

What are those limiting beliefs? Know that they didn't start with you. These are all the things you heard, witnessed, and experienced firsthand, starting from childhood. At the same time, your brain created the beliefs and then sifted through the information available to find supporting evidence for the beliefs you created. These conscious and unconscious limiting beliefs become your subjective perception of reality — your internal ecosystem that affects how you live your life.

Beliefs lead to your expectations, and your results align with that. Start looking at all your beliefs and question where they came from. Once you do, you can begin to rewrite your story and make progress toward your writing goals.

2. Set a small, manageable, achievable writing goal with a clear deadline.

Like a loyal yellow Lab, your unconscious mind is there for you — it's doing what it thinks you want it to do because you've been at it for so long. What you're about to do is show your unconscious mind that you're going to be rocking this writing thing differently — you have an upgraded program running now!

Positive rewards and reinforcement can help here too. Going back to the memoir writing example, let's say we'll set a small, reasonable goal of writing three hundred words a day. And once you achieve that after a period of time — say over three weeks, you can easily slide up to five hundred words, then one thousand, and grow from there.

And I'm being extra-conservative here. Your unconscious mind will catch on so quickly that you can probably get there in less time. By consistently increasing your goal even by a few hundred words each week, your unconscious mind will get on board fast, making it easier for you to write more.

The key is to increase the goal consistently. Here's a sample schedule:

- Week 1: 2,100 words
- Week 2: 2,100 words
- Week 3: 2,100 words

- Week 4: +500 words a day, so 3,500 words
- Week 5: 3,500 words
- Week 6: 3,500 words . . . and so on

This is how I help my clients assemble their bodies of content, write their websites, and make progress on their books. It's only possible when the goal is believable to your conscious and unconscious minds.

You've heard of the SMART goal framework — and if you're rolling your eyes, I get it — I used to roll my eyes too. According to NLP, a good goal is "smarter":

Specific, **S**imple, and you can see yourself doing it.
Measurable and **M**eaningful to you — meaning leads to motivation.
Achievable, as of now, and will benefit all areas of life.
Realistic, **R**esponsible, and ecological.
Time is involved and **T**oward what you want.

Here's an example of writing your goal using positive, "toward language" to describe what you want:

By December 1, I'll have written at least three hundred words every single day on my book project joyfully and easily. Bringing with it a tremendous amount of happiness, satisfaction, abundance, and flow. Thank you, thank you, thank you.

Always close your goal with gratitude.

3. Talk about your goal in terms of what you *want*, not what you *don't want*.

You're going to talk about your goal a lot, so use positive language that will support you in getting this goal. The conscious use of language is critical. NLP calls this "toward language," because it's moving you toward your goal. When you learn to use toward language consciously with the words you speak and write, you'll have a better chance of using toward language internally.

This is important because the unconscious mind doesn't process negatives. If you say, "I don't want to get sick," your brain hears, "Get sick." This is an example of away-from language. You're talking about what you want in the context of it being the opposite of what you don't want. Toward language would be: "I'm staying healthy." Your mind hears, "Stay healthy." So many people overlook these nuances that support our success.

Here's an example of how it works with writing goals:

- Away-from language: "I'm writing a book, and holy shitballs, is it exhausting. I'm only consuming bread and coffee. I don't know what I'm doing, but I know I don't want to do what I was doing before. This is hard and I'm worried I'll never finish this thing."
- Toward language: "I'm writing a book, and it's stretching me in so many ways I never imagined. It will take time, and I'm dedicated to making it work."

Away-from thinking — like complaining, or resisting people, work, and situations — can deliver more of it to your life. Your internal dialogue has a huge impact on your state, and it's these things that create the negative internal representations — internal pictures that your brain uses to communicate, that create the negative states.

4. Focus on the very last step of your writing goal.

Focus on the final step, i.e., the task or event that would happen to let you know you've met your writing goal. Perhaps it's proofreading the final draft of your book before it goes to print or holding the print proof in your hands. This is unique to you.

How will you know when you've realized your goal? Internalize that precise moment by fully immersing yourself in what it looks like, feels like, sounds like, and even smells like. Look at where you'll be sitting in your home or workspace when it happens. Doing this internalization tells your unconscious mind to expect success — and equally, the exercise will show you the essence of what you focus on. You'll start seeing synchronicities that align with your focus, giving you the encouragement to keep going.

And here's a small but important distinction: First, see it through your own eyes, as if you're in your body right now, looking outward into your environment. Once you get the internal visual where you want it, imagine jumping out of the image, so you see your body from the outside in the picture. This creates a direction for the unconscious mind to go — consider it a GPS for the unconscious mind.

The final stage is to take a small, doable action step in the direction of your writing goal. For instance, write your three hundred words every morning before diving into other work. Your unconscious mind thrives on repetition, so visualizing this success every morning and every night before you go to sleep is like playing a movie in your mind on repeat. Rename your alarm something like, "Wake up, beautiful author!" to remind you of your goal. Just like when you watched a movie you loved as a kid repeatedly and learned the lines without even trying, this is what's happening with your unconscious mind.

Pay close attention to your emotions and lean into them. Really *feel* into them as deeply as you can.

The magic of working with your unconscious mind in this way is that as you take action toward your writing goal — every time you sit down to the page or successfully write for a Pomodoro sprint (see Chapter 3) — you'll start to see more things showing up in your life to help and support you in reaching your goal.

I just love watching the magic that happens inside this process as I gain momentum. As I was working on my memoir, I started attracting some next-level copywriting clients — I was in awe at the work I was doing. I was also drawn to healing work, which led me to eat more fresh, raw, life-giving foods, which led to feeling clearer and stronger. People in my writing community also announced they were working on their memoirs. You're likely going to see it in all areas of your life. And that is some motherfucking magic.

5. Write at the same time and/or the same place to create an anchor.

Writing routines and rituals help make writing easier. Just like having a regular bedtime (and bed to sleep in) supports your healthy sleeping habits, when you write in that same spot on the left side of the couch, your unconscious mind will know this is the time and place to write and will support you in creating the environmental conditions to make it happen. After a time, your body just knows it's time to write. If you try writing in the spot where you're usually scrolling the internet, your brain could have a harder time getting on board with what you want it to do. Or suppose you have ripe avocados next to your sprouted grain bread on the counter. You see these right as you're boiling water for your morning cup of tea. Your brain just knows, "It's time to have some avocado toast!" Read more about rituals in Chapter 11.

YOU'VE REACHED YOUR GOAL – NOW WHAT?

When you've reached your goal, relish, with all your senses, how good it feels. Pause to celebrate and savor that win to the max. Then when you're ready to come back to work, set a bigger goal, and repeat the process. You finish your memoir, celebrate, then start your next book, or launch a new business, or finish your website copy. Success breeds success. This is how you make small changes and see significant results – and usually in less time than you'd imagine.

Deciding to make a deliberate change and going after big results involves marrying your conscious and unconscious minds. Choose logically with your conscious brain and, to get the message into the unconscious mind, take baby steps – believable, attainable baby steps.

As I wrote this book, I planted seeds in my mind of what I'd write about the next day.

- At the end of each workday, I'd look at the topic for the next day. I'd quickly review my notes and then put them away. That's *it*.
- Then, first thing in the morning, I'd bring that topic to mind and let my mind wander. It wasn't about forcing or making it happen, but rather letting my unconscious mind do the work. This way, when I came to the page, I'd already been rolling the idea around. This is also another sneaky way to move past resistance.

- Because the ideas had been reverberating in my brain for a while, I'd be excited to get to the page. I was itching to let all the words out.

Intuitive Writing Tip

Play a little brain game and write about one topic a week, whether it's for your blog or a book chapter. On the weekend before you write, review your notes and think about what you want to say without trying to get any of the words down. Over time, you're training your unconscious mind to do the heavy lifting for you.

SURROUND YOURSELF WITH PEOPLE WHO ENERGIZE YOU

Once you plant these seeds in your mind, you'll start noticing people showing up who can support you. It's just like when you buy a Jeep Wrangler and you notice all the other Jeeps on the road, then suddenly you even see that they're waving at you. (I wondered why people started waving at us all the time once we got a Jeep. I learned it was a Jeep thing.)

The same goes for other things. You get what you focus on. If you're focused on being an intuitive, laid-back writer, guess what you're going to get? Everywhere you go you'll likely meet more cool AF people who like writing — people who are setting writing goals and following through on them.

If you look around you and the people you're surrounded by are complaining, using negative language, and not doing what they say they're going to do, consider running as fast as you can in the other direction. They're hindering, not helping, your process. If you're the average of the five people with whom you keep company, consider what kinds of people they are. If you're keeping company with others whose biggest goal is to tweet six times a day, criticize an author's work, or gossip, it's going to be even more challenging to raise yourself up to the badass intuitive writer you know you can be.

Instead, start looking for more positive people. And good news — if you've been focusing on your feel-good writing practice, you're naturally going to attract some other high-vibing friends.

The business owners who have the most success in my writing community are the ones who show up to writing sessions regularly, participate in the workshops, and revisit the templates. These intuitive writers get the most writing done, publish books, launch their businesses, leave day jobs, and create the most content. They're actively creating for themselves the most supportive environment in which to achieve what they want.

If you wanted to start running but were more acquainted with the local pub and your sofa, you might try a couch-to-5K running program, something you're not going to do with your buddies from the local bar. You might need some running friends or, at the very least, you might benefit from seeing your drinking friends less often while you work on your fitness goals.

We're meant to connect with others, and the more we can do that around a common goal, the more likely it will be that we reach our goals — and the more satisfying it will be when we do. Surrounding ourselves with like-minded people who want similar things gives us a deep sense of compassion toward one another. We're in it together and understand what we're all going through.

MANIFEST EVERYTHING YOUR WRITER SOUL DESIRES

If you think manifesting is woo-woo BS, hear me out. We know that everything is energy.

What we focus on expands. If you focus on writer's block, your unconscious mind will focus on the essence of being blocked — and deliver more blocks to you in many areas of your life. Focus on creativity, flow, and the endless well of ideas and you'll get just that — limitless inspiration.

It sounds simple because it is — it just requires constant practice. And it's not only the words you use out loud; the ones you use in your head are just as important.

Remember we want to focus on what we want using positive, toward language, speaking it into existence as if it's here and real today.

When I wanted to leave my corporate job and go full-time in my copywriting business, I focused on how good it would feel to be running my business. Each morning when I woke up, I'd imagine I was getting ready to go work in my home office, doing writing I loved for amazing clients, even though in my 3D life, I was getting dressed at 6:00 a.m. to commute over an hour to sit in a grey cubicle.

With my growing side hustle, I'd imagine that I did freelance writing work all day. When doing the work required of my 9-to-5, I felt the emotions I'd feel working in my business.

I bathed in the feel-good, positive emotions that being my own boss would bring. I also did fun things like changing all my passwords to remind me of my goals constantly. As an example, one password could be "BeMyOwnBada$$BOSSin2017." Every time I'd key in my password, I'd remember my objective.

Meet my friend, Roxana, who's manifesting a career as an author. The following is a peek into her personal manifesting process.

> "The process starts with me deciding what I genuinely want and getting real about what I desire. Then I look to my reality and clear up any

limiting beliefs that come up. I then write my new rules for reality — things that must be true for that desire to be a part of my entire reality. I'm rewriting old beliefs continually.

I'm consciously choosing beliefs around my writing and career as an author. This gives me several mantras I replay in my head. I record my voice reading through them and then listen to that audio at least daily. I also create subliminal audio and play it in the background sometimes when I'm just working on other stuff.

Here are some of my mantras as an example:

I am on the path to becoming a published author.

I easily find time to write every day.

It's easy for me to edit my book.

I complete the third draft of my book right on time.

I am infinitely supported in my journey toward signing a book deal.

I am infinitely supported in my book writing career.

My ideal publisher and I are destined for each other.

I allow my book to be bought by the ideal publisher.

Thank you, Source, for aligning such a perfect book deal for me!

You can see that Roxana's manifesting process is quite simple. Create your own list of mantras or feel-good statements to repeat about what *you* want your writing to look like. Use words you'd actually use. You want these statements to feel believable to your unconscious mind.

FUTURE-STATE JOURNALING

Because all my actions are either supporting or hindering my success, I wanted to weave some manifesting practices into my morning pages habit. I decided to wrap them up on a feel-good note to support my goals. To be clear, this isn't something that Julia Cameron recommends in *The Artist's Way* when talking about morning pages — it's *my* spin.

Now, as I near the end of my three pages of stream-of-consciousness writing, I switch gears to writing about the one big writing goal I'm focused on at the time. I'll start with something that looks like the samples below to kick it off, then I'll keep going deeper into that visual, writing on the following questions:

What does it look like when I'm done?

Where am I doing all this writing?

Where do I live?

What am I wearing?

What's in my cup?

How am I celebrating?

Don't force an idea of what it needs to look like — just start writing whatever comes to mind as you're focusing on your future state.

Write it as if it's here today.

Here are some examples:

I'm so happy and grateful that I easily and joyfully manifested a beautiful book with a deep blue cover. Seeing this book out in the world brings tremendous joy, abundance, and prosperity. Thank you, thank you, thank you.

Then, keep going with what you see, sense, and feel — as if it's true today, right in the present moment.

JOURNAL PROMPTS

To practice this tool, here are some writing prompts to help connect with your unconscious mind:

1. Tap back into that visualization you do each morning and evening. How do you *feel* as an entrepreneur sending a newsletter?
2. How do you *feel* as a business owner publishing a blog post?
3. How do you *feel* with a memoir ready to go out into the world?
4. How do you *feel* when you set a goal and take small actions, bit by bit, until you get there? Sink into those feelings.
5. What feelings and emotions are present as you complete the final step before realizing your writing goal?

CHAPTER 10
HEALING YOUR WOUNDS FOR BETTER WRITING

After returning to that shiny corporate boardroom after my first maternity leave, wondering what the hell I was doing there, I had the deep knowing that I was meant for more — I just needed help seeing what that was.

This led me to where most seekers find themselves — the self-development section of the bookstore. I read a lot and quickly opened my eyes to new ways of thinking, rewriting old stories, and adopting new beliefs.

Even though I was creating positive change on the inside, I still had trouble speaking up and writing what was on my heart.

I believed I didn't have anything important to say, so I'd sit quiet — a lot. At times, I felt like I was different — sheltered, perhaps, in my middle-class Toronto suburb, and highly privileged.

Even when I started doing breakthrough work and hypnosis to dive deeper into the stories I'd tell in *Unfussy Life*, it brought up even more awkward questions.

Who am I to tell these stories?

Who even cares?

Do I have anything important to say?

I'd later learn that these are the inner critic voices that darkness uses to keep us stuck, small — and especially quiet.

Quiet . . . now that struck a chord.

I distinctly remember family events where relatives would comment on how quiet I was. Sometimes they'd tell me that I was sitting so still that I looked like a statue. For me, being invisible was safer because no one could criticize me if they couldn't see me.

Speak when you're spoken to.

Only say something when you have something nice to say.

Everyone will look at you.

Speaking up and even speaking, in general, was challenging for me. Even today, I much prefer the comfort of a notebook to work out how I feel about something. I like to know what I think before opening my mouth.

Early in my management consulting career, I had to speak a lot. I'd be nervous and would sometimes stumble over my words. Especially when I feared I had made a mistake or would be called out for doing something wrong. I had to do enough big presentations that it forced me to overcome those fears relatively quickly. But I was speaking on my company's behalf and sharing their truth — not mine.

Then it came time to share my truths. One of the very first posts I published when I had a plant-based food blog was about how I took my then sixteen-month-old son off dairy to avoid an unnecessary tonsillectomy. It worked. And in publishing that first piece, I worried about offending people — all those who did have their tonsils out, those who still drank cow's milk.

Those fears were unfounded — no one said shitty things.

Occasionally, however, I'd write something that triggered someone. Like when a relative didn't like a blog post suggesting that men in corporate drop their ties and wear what they're comfortable in. This relative told me I was too harsh and that she was offended because her husband had to wear a tie to work.

There will always be haters who don't like what you have to say. You're not writing for the critics — you're writing for your fans.

I'm glad these experiences didn't stop me from writing. My writing will always offend someone. It isn't for everyone. It's for the people who need to read it.

Wealthy, happy, and successful people will likely never criticize you. We'll talk more about this in Chapter 23. In essence, we're projecting our insecurities and doubts onto the people who spew those negative comments. Even a slightly negative comment can cause most writers to freeze up.

My throat chakra seemed to be open for writing, but when it came to speaking, I wasn't there yet.

A few short years ago, I'd be on Zoom calls with clients or in a group, and someone would say something that didn't sit well with me. I had something to say. First, I'd notice my heart rate rise. Then, I'd become acutely aware that my neck was so stiff that I was worried about moving it out of fear that it would creak so loud that everyone on the call would hear it. It wasn't a trigger — it was that I had a truth to share: a knowing, a personal experience, something that was only mine to share.

I'd often mute myself and stretch my neck from side to side, relieving the pressure. That worked in the moment, but I wouldn't speak up later either. I wasn't actually doing the work to heal yet, so I left much unsaid.

I was keeping my stories to myself. Keeping them locked deep inside where no one could hear them.

While deep in revisions of *Unfussy Life*, while that inner voice whispered in my ear, "No one wants to read your stories," I had a dream that jolted me awake. My heart pounding, I looked around the room to make sure I was still alive.

In the dream, I was attempting to speak. Except the words didn't come. I opened my mouth — and nothing. When the words wouldn't come, I grasped my throat, eyes wide in horror. I couldn't speak. At that moment, I realized that not speaking up meant death.

By not speaking, I was dying. I sank into the bed and through to the first floor, into death, where I knew I would cease to exist.

When I woke up, I saw my husband next to me and realized it was all a dream. Phew!

Now, I've had plenty of dreams about losing teeth and walking into school without pants (more than I care to admit), but the no-voice thing — this was new. That dream catalyzed me. I recommitted to finishing the book and self-published it a few months later.

The only thing that would eventually relieve the creaky neck? Beginning the *real* healing work.

It was late 2020, and a business connection shared a spiritual teacher's insights into what was really going on in the world. When I read her posts, I felt a deep knowing that it was truth. Everything clicked — it just made sense. My body knew.

Learning more about her started me down an even deeper healing path. I signed up for some of her healing programs. Holy shit, was I in for an eye-opening. I had been glossing over and bypassing in so many areas of my life. When you start doing real healing work, previously buried experiences bubble up to the surface to be healed.

When I was digging into my past while writing *Unfussy Life*, truths started emerging. Healing is ongoing. I'm not finished. I circled back to do more with my breakthrough coach right around the time of finalizing edits to this book. This is lifelong work — which is also why so many quit or don't even start. I've healed a lot of shit and still have work to do.

When you start healing, there's an upside-down-ness to how you see life. It can take everything you think you know and show you just how wrong you've been.

But then, you can rebuild and begin to move through life with less resistance. Because I started doing deep healing work before I started writing this book, the words you read in here flowed like nothing else. Writing while healing? Ten out of ten recommend.

I learned that many people have blocked throat chakras and this affects their writing, making it feel controlled, stifled, and forced. Just the kind of writing that made me decide to start teaching intuitive writing.

I focused on healing my throat chakra by finally speaking up whenever the urge struck. I also stopped looking for answers outside myself and threw out my oracle cards, stopped consulting reiki and tarot practitioners, and focused on nurturing my pineal gland and opening my third eye, where I had a lot of stuck energy.

While throat chakra healing had the most direct effect on my writing, healing core wounds like abandonment, rejection, guilt, and shame are all in there too. We all have these wounds. Just remember, they're *wounds* — which means you can heal them. You're not broken, you just need some love.

Intuitive Writing Tip

Healing work is life work. Be gentle with yourself as you heal and write.

This intentional work is opening up deeper layers in my writing that I didn't sense there before. I can still feel it all unfolding, and while I tend to want to rush the process, I know I need to surrender and trust.

Now, my neck doesn't creak when I have something to say.

My throat is open when it's time to speak. I might feel like puking, but I say what I need to say anyway.

Bit by bit, the more we speak, write, and share our truths, the more we clear ourselves.

Speaking up when I'm called has opened up so much more for me. I feel clear, more creative, and even more like myself. Completely congruent and aligned.

Now, I want you to meet Malana. She shares in her own words how trauma and abuse impacted her voice and creativity.

When I was eleven years old, I went mute.

It was the summer before sixth grade, and one morning, I woke up with memories of things I didn't understand. Things that brought me deep shame and suffocating guilt.

And hard as I tried, I couldn't bring myself to speak.

The worst of it lasted several months. A few words here and there. But not at all what I wanted to say. And no one urged me to talk. I'd even follow my mother around and squeak out a little "M-mom?" And then I'd stop. And she didn't ask. She didn't probe.

For the next two decades, I experienced blocks in everything from my confidence, to my career, to my communication, and to my creativity. And even though I had a zest for life and an affinity for looking on the bright side, I gravitated toward things that would hold me prisoner and keep me mired in darkness.

Things like . . .

The weed that would give me twenty minutes

of manic euphoria before leaving me feeling scattered and fatigued.

The alcohol, toxic food, and lack of exercise that kept me numb, inflamed, and lethargic.

The families — both the one I was born into and the one I had married into — that were rife with dysfunction and addiction.

The marriage where I was reduced to an object and spent more time shouldering their burdens and battles while barely being able to shoulder my own.

All things that would zap my energy, my drive, and my focus. Because . . .

I wasn't creating much if I was drunk, high, or being drained by a man.

And worst of all, I wasn't digging deep into why I felt so damn BLOCKED in the first place.

However, when it came to my creativity, I did find a loophole. It came through working with other creatives. I'd keep busy behind the scenes of their businesses, while telling myself, 'Hey, I'm doing great work using my talents, gifts, and skills to share other people's messages. And that matters! So I'm good . . . right?'

But I wasn't good, and it wasn't right.

I was sad, sick, and lonely. I was in pain. I could literally feel myself wasting my life away. There were days when I just wanted to *scream* at the top of my lungs in frustration!

Instead, I'd get high.

And I'd think, "*Today* is the day I'll have the best idea, ever! And I'll take action on it! And I'll help tons of people while making tons of money! I've *got* this!"

I really did have some good ideas, too. Great ones, even. And I'd take some action. Sometimes I'd even share these ideas and actions with others. Like a poem, painting, or new dish. Then I'd fizzle out.

And I'd return to client work where it was easier, safer, and I didn't have to dig any deeper. I could just hide.

My life became a collection of half-baked writings, unfinished paintings, the odd poem, a vision board collecting dust, and a burning desire to do *something*.

Then 2020 came and shook me awake.

As the world changed on the outside, I began to change on the inside. All of a sudden, nothing became more important to me than freedom – something I'd realized I'd taken for granted, and it hit me: "*Wait!* Don't take it away! I've barely lived yet!"

This realization brought me profound grief and sadness, but it was also a catalyst for some of the most important changes I would make in my life.

One of them was finally facing my addiction to weed, and by the end of that year, after ten years of almost daily use, I was finally ready to let it go.

I was led to the exact teacher and support I needed to help me kick my addiction for good and detox my body from years of self-abuse. Just a few months after that, I was 100 percent sober.

I could now go more deeply into my spiritual healing and get to the root of *why* I'd been using weed for ten years.

Which took me right back to being eleven years old and waking up to the memories of things I didn't understand.

To the sexual abuse I'd experienced at the hands of the man who was supposed to love me the most.

And there it was.

The link between my trauma and my creativity, my endless frustration, my affinity for drugs, my terrible choices in men, and my constant desire to be, have, and do more, yet feeling like I was on a constant hamster wheel to nowhere.

As I look back at the years I spent fumbling around in the dark, I now know that carrying the weight of trauma and abuse of all kinds molded me into someone who felt unworthy, someone who felt like she had to hide from the world out of guilt and shame, someone who felt "marked" and wrong for wanting to shine. Someone who felt she had to settle in her marriage, in her health, in her career – in everything.

It wasn't until I was finally willing to get real about how I was living my life, started taking better care of, and truly listening to, my body and my intuition, and learned how to be there for myself in a way that no one else had ever been, that I could finally have a chance at living the full, creative life I deserved.

It's been over a year since I healed my drug addiction and got to the root of why I'd gone

> mute, and since then, I've stood up to my abusers, started a new career, moved to a beautiful location I'd always dreamed of, ended my toxic marriage, and I've been writing and creating regularly – without the high.
>
> Trauma and abuse left unhealed prevents us from doing, being, and achieving our very best in life. It did for me. But once I mustered up the courage to clear away the darkness from my life and dedicate myself to healing my mind, body, and spirit, nothing and no one can shut me up, shut me down, or stop me now. I now know that I was put on this earth to shine in my own unique way, and now, I truly can.

Now, Malana is free to shine.

CLEARING THE WAY FOR CREATIVITY

When I was halfway through editing my last book, *Unfussy Life*, I started working with my NLP breakthrough coach. I uncovered all kinds of gunk in my brain – limiting beliefs, old stories that weren't serving me, and wounding from lifetimes past, present, and parallel – wounding that we all have in some form or another.

Right before publishing that book, I went deep into excavating things that happened to me when I was younger that I didn't even recall initially. Slowly, over time, more and more was revealed to me. Here I want to tell you that *shit came up* while I was working on that big writing project – and may come up for you. I share this with you for two reasons. First, so you can see that doing deep healing work didn't derail my mission to get my writing out there. And second, that writing opened me up to doing the deep healing work.

The good news is: writing can still happen when your bruises are fading. You can heal your wounds and do deep, profound healing work, including journeying to past lives, ancestors' timelines, and childhood to uncover and heal what happened.

Why would you want to do this and not just leave shit alone?

Because clarity is key to healing – every wound you uncover and heal makes you a clearer vessel for sharing light and tuning into your intuition. I uncovered wounds I didn't know I had and likely will continue to discover more.

This is part of the work of being a human on this planet. And it's my responsibility as a writer to write from as clear a place as possible. As I change and evolve, I look back at my writing and see how much ego was present. I was writing from a place of unawareness – certain parts of me had been hiding in the shadow.

While my instinct may be to unpublish all that old work, that would also be irresponsible. I leave it there to show my evolution. And because I trust that some readers may resonate with older work of mine and not the new stuff based on their unique path and where they are right now.

PART THREE

CLAIMING YOUR INTUITIVE WRITING PRACTICE

You're either writing or not writing. It's time to put your stake in the ground and claim your intuitive writing practice. When you follow the practical and just plain fun suggestions in this section, your writing will begin to feel good — really good. And when your writing life feels good, the rest of your life turns to magic.

CHAPTER 11
INTUITIVE WRITERS CREATE GOOD HABITS

People often ask me, "How do you do it all?"

They're particularly likely to ask me this when they see that I put a lot of writing out each year, maintain a full client roster, and support active kids in sports that involve lots of travel.

Truthfully, I kind of hate this question. Because I actually don't do it "all." Let's remember that anytime you read something online that someone has written about their own life, you're getting a glimpse at the highlight reel of that life. So, in my case, for example, you're not seeing the bare fridge or the vacuum cleaner that's been sitting in the middle of the living room for a week — when no actual vacuuming has been taking place.

We can only juggle so many balls before we drop all of them. On any given day, for me that juggle includes writing, reading, cooking, shuttling the kids around while they live their best lives, spending time with them, painting, blogging, coaching, editing, speaking, publishing books, and still finding time to enjoy life. I do have lots to get done in a day, but you'll never hear me say, "I'm busy," because I don't think it's a particularly useful or empowering phrase to use.

What you will hear me say, quite often, is "No."

I say no to a lot of things. I'm at home much of the time, and I'm often heads-down working on what matters most to me and taking care of kid-related things. Those are, in order:

- health and healing
- family and relationships
- business

These are the priorities I choose in the name of embracing my greatness and giving the middle finger to mediocrity.

I didn't always have this kind of clarity, though.

I eventually got clear on my priorities after struggling with the distractions and time-sucks that most of us deal with. You know how it goes: settle in on the couch after a long day of Zoom calls, flip on Netflix with your laptop perched on your knees — with every intention of doing some work while you watch *Cobra Kai*. Then your phone buzzes with a text from a friend.

You wrap up your phone call and since you have your phone in hand, you scroll. More scrolling . . . and more . . . scrolling.

Until you catch yourself after who knows how long, thinking, "How the hell did I get here? And what am I even watching on TV — how did that guy get in there, and why is he clinking glasses with that creepy dude with the ponytail?"

Even after taking intentional pauses from electronic media in the past, deleting accounts and reactivating them, removing and reinstalling apps on my phone, I can still find myself in the scrolling trap. I track my time for every business activity, and yet, somehow, I end up back at this place of consuming more than I'm creating.

Not putting my body, health, and family first.

And, most importantly, not writing.

I'll go into a book editing session and think, "Oh, let me just check Instagram first."

Um. Check it for *what* exactly?

Swap this out for any platform — Telegram, Signal, or text messaging.

What I'm really doing is sabotaging myself from the uncomfortable work of starting, digging in, going deep, and eventually finishing.

Important projects keep nagging at me, and yet here I am again, choosing the comfortable thing in the moment — doing nothing.

Here's what I do to break the cycle:

I remind myself why finishing my writing project is so darn important to me. And I face the fact that letting the project sit in a Google Doc while I play in the tech world of distraction and make-believe isn't going to get the book out into the hands of those I'm writing it for.

I tell myself I've come too far on the project to be goofing off for even thirty minutes a day on social media. If I want to focus on creating excellence in all areas of my life, I need to revisit my daily habits.

Creating before jumping into social media is only one example of a practice I adopted, and it got me thinking of all the other ways I could stay in the "flow zone" — where I'm most effective and doing the work that will improve my life, my family, or my business.

At the end of the day and the end of my life, I want to say I persevered toward greatness.

Please know that the pursuit of excellence doesn't mean

I'm always on or that my life is free of shit-show moments or failures. There are still plenty of those.

Persevering means I care. I care about my work – getting better at it and serving my clients in more powerful ways. By committing to excellence, I can do that – with less pushing and more ease.

Let's talk about productive writing habits that can support you in getting the most writing done, in the most painless way possible. The fun part about this kind of habit-building is that you'll actually start to enjoy the writing process more.

The best way to get into the writing habit is not to think about it too much. When we think about the things we don't want to do, it's too easy to simply not do them. We need to get out of thinking and into feeling – letting our hearts lead the way.

CREATE A RITUAL

Rituals can help get us into our bodies, and this makes the process of starting and continuing to write easier.

Introducing a ritual in your writing practice helps create an effortless habit. And once you've initiated the practice, you build momentum. You know, when you're "in the zone" or "in the flow" and you're not consciously aware that you're working, writing, painting, or whatever it is? It's that feeling when you just can't stop. It's as if you don't have a body. That's the state of creation we're striving for here, friend.

Here are some examples of rituals. Use these ideas to inspire your own:

1. When I wrote my first mini-book, I created a music playlist called "write the book." Every time I had scheduled to write and edit, I started the playlist

from the beginning. When "Believe" by Mumford and Sons started playing, my body knew it was time to write. Some days, I'd play the song on repeat to keep my brain and my fingers moving.

2. When I sit down with my cacao latte each morning, it's time to start book edits.
3. Creating different music playlists for different kinds of work — when I'm writing for copywriting clients, I'll play calm music for the yoga instructors and hard rock for the badass coaches. If I'm writing for a client, I'll write along to the music they'd listen to. If you find music distracting, use classical music or cue up a specific song before you begin, just to get you into the zone, and then turn it off when it's time to write.
4. What's your arena song? When NHL players jump onto the ice at the start of a game, they play a song to get them pumped up. What music makes you want to get up and go? Play that right before you start writing, and when the song ends, dive right in.
5. Writing feels like a sacred practice of grounding into my creativity and going inward. I start every writing session by lighting a candle. When I break for lunch, I put it out and then relight it when I return to my desk.
6. Keep a particular scent of lip balm on your desk and put it on right before you begin.
7. Diffuse essential oils in your writing space or just keep them nearby to sniff — some good scents could be lemon, mint, frankincense, or lavender. Of course, use something you enjoy and play with your own blends.
8. Dab some perfume on before you write.

9. A book editor I know puts on red lipstick and slides her hair into a top bun to get into her zone.
10. Use a facial spray to lightly mist your face before you begin your writing practice.
11. Get dressed for writing — every day. What does intuitive-writer-you wear? I set this habit early on in my entrepreneur days. When I spend five minutes putting a little makeup on and grooming, I'm much more productive than I am in sweats and an unwashed face.
12. Set your intentions each morning and night. Every night before bed, express gratitude for how the next day went — that's right — past tense, like it already happened, and it was amazing. Try it! And then do the same in the morning, setting the stage for a great day.

Here are some additional tips to help get you started on your ritual creation:

Notice the daily habits you already have. Is there a "trigger" that makes them happen? Maybe you hear your alarm, grab your sneakers, and head out for a run; or you finish dinner and brew some tea. Link a solid habit you already have with writing.

Make a list of things you enjoy doing and already do: walks, dancing, eating chocolate. Take one of those things and schedule it to immediately follow some writing time. Take a thirty minute walk then write for sixty minutes. Turn on your favorite music, write a blog post. Take a sip of tea, start working through email.

When you're able to simply start, momentum takes over, and you'll probably find you're able to get more done. Keep in mind, this isn't about crossing stuff off your to-do list like a crazed taskmaster; it's about prioritizing the things you want to accomplish.

Give your rituals a makeover throughout the year. Maybe summer writing looks different from winter writing. Your writing habits when the kids go back to school in the fall likely look different from vacation writing. This is not to say that you need to write while on vacation. The whole point of designing a writing life you enjoy is that you don't need a break from it. If it becomes part of your life, it'll be easier to stay in the zone, you'll want to write, and you'll be more likely to have more time working in flow.

That said, take breaks. You need rest. And your writing practice will thank you. Visit Chapter 13 and notice where you need rest — and honor that.

WHERE YOU WRITE

You might enjoy different settings for different projects. Most of the work on my books happens while I'm not at my desk. If you're having trouble getting started, try picking up and moving to another spot in your home.

I did a lot of book writing on the couch and in an Adirondack chair on my porch. These settings helped me view my writing sessions as more creative and less business-centered. I'd write on the couch and edit at my desk because editing means business — that, and because having a big monitor makes it easier on my eyes.

If you have kids in activities, you'll find lots of opportunities for writing to happen in the cracks of life. I've spent many hours writing and editing in frigid hockey arenas and in piano lesson waiting rooms. Instead of scrolling on my phone mindlessly, I look for every possible opportunity to make progress on my writing. Or, I'll invest the time in listening to an audiobook and perhaps making notes while I integrate the lessons.

Intuitive Writing Tip
Create a few designated spots for writing in your home and invest some time in making them beautiful.

Mary, a friend and former client, used to struggle with writing and sharing her work until she created a feel-good writing experience.

> My work used to be completely in-person. So before launching my first online program, I felt anxious about putting myself out there and sharing my ideas in a new way. Adding to the pressure, I had a tight deadline because I was about to unplug and go on a retreat.
>
> Jacq and I spent a fall afternoon in a Boston hotel lobby, comfortably settled in heavy library chairs surrounded by abundant floor-to-ceiling bookshelves. I cozied into a nook by the fire, wearing slippers (yes, in the hotel lobby) and a blanket to warm my bones.
>
> I felt so held by Jacq through that experience.
>
> In many ways, it was an initiation. Going into this program launch, I'd seen many entrepreneurial circles make launching an online program look like this massive fucking thing. I thought it was supposed to be complicated and if I wasn't anxious, I must be doing it wrong.
>
> By following the intuitive writing process Jacq walked me through, I found a palpable — and surprising — sense of freedom in business writing.

> Creating an email sequence to sell my program was such an easy, fluid experience. I didn't know that writing could feel like that. This situation could have been stressful because I had to get my emails all sorted and automated in such a short timeframe.
>
> But sitting down with a cup of tea by a fire in a hotel and writing and launching a program was so fucking easy.
>
> Ever since that day, whenever I'm writing and I feel like I'm getting stuck, or that self-editing voice comes in, I go back to what it felt like to feel the ease and the freedom of self-expression and how easy it can be to communicate and just write.
>
> That day, I created a visceral experience of that freedom. I return to that kinesthetic in my body every time I write now. It's transformed how I work. Anytime I notice tension or rigidity creeping into my writing, I take a break and go back to the cozy fire that crisp afternoon and remember how easy it can be when there's freedom and joy in the process.

When you create freedom during the writing process, it becomes a nurturing act of self-care.

JOURNAL PROMPTS

1. What choices will you make in the name of writing greatness? Make a list and refer back to it daily.
2. Bring a feel-good writing session from the past to mind. Where were you? What were you doing

right before and after? What were you wearing? What did you see in front of you? Describe the scene in detail. You can go back to this scene in your mind before you begin each writing session.

3. As you begin writing, consider how you want to feel when you're finished. Take a few seconds and journal about what it feels like to be finished for the day.
4. Do your writing habits look different in the future? Describe how they look. Does future you have writing habits that aren't reasonable for your life right now? Hold that vision as you're writing today. If you're a visual person, create a vision board depicting your ideal writing space.

CHAPTER 12
INTUITIVE INSPIRATION

I used to find the idea of writing overwhelming. I realized it was because I was pouring all the pieces of the creation process into one six-hundred-pound bucket that was impossible to carry. That bucket held topic ideas, writing, when to write, editing, posting, promoting — a slurry of things that really needed separate containers.

When people ask me how they can be a more productive writer, I ask them about their process and it almost always turns out they're editing while they write. I get it — I used to naively aim to sit down and write a final draft all in one go. Holy shit, that's challenging! No wonder so many people aren't writing as much as they want. It's just too much effort.

Writing that way is nearly impossible, takes extra fuel, and uses up all kinds of energy in our brains.

Here, we'll look at your writing project in four distinct phases. While most of our creative work moves progressively through these phases, sometimes our work flows upstream and downstream rather than in a fully linear fashion.

Intuitive Inspiration
Intuitive Planning
Intuitive Creation
Intuitive Editing & Refining

INTUITIVE INSPIRATION

This is where the ideas come in. And inspiration comes in waves. The water might be totally still or it might come in fast and furious with a category-five storm surge.

Tidal-wave-type inspiration can leave us with that feeling of squirrel brain, where we don't know which ideas to choose. If you're overwhelmed with inspiration and can't pick one of your twelve thousand ideas to focus on, you wind up sitting and doing nothing.

The other end of the spectrum might have you in front of the blank page with a looming deadline. Perhaps you promised a blog post, a weekly email newsletter, or a new poem to your audience. If you've got no ideas and no inspiration is coming in, you wind up sitting and doing nothing

Or worse, you sit there and force something out, feeling agitated and frustrated, and it falls flat with your audience. You spent hours writing it. So then you think to yourself, "What a waste that was!" Then you stop blogging or emailing altogether. Yikes.

The other mistake I've made, and I see plenty of other creatives making this same one, is feeling desperate and looking to social media for inspiration in the moment. Social media isn't a place to look for inspiration when it's time to write. What it *is* is a trap — a black hole of bullshit time-wasters with tiny slivers of pure light. Its only design is to keep you there longer. You'll definitely find plenty of inspiration on social channels. But you need to go in there at a time separate from when you want to write. Keep your scrolling and connecting time separate from designated inspiration time.

Another way to gather more inspiration is to look at images of your subject matter, as mentioned in Chapter 3. This will unlock new ideas if you feel stuck.

It's hard to feel inspired, though, if your head is filled with everyone else's ideas and you never take a moment to integrate what you've learned and figure out which ideas are yours.

So, another way to seek inspiration without the clutter of other people's ideas is to get a change of scenery, aka travel — even if only to the next town over or a different café. This fresh perspective can reveal new ideas you didn't know you had.

A NOTE ABOUT INSPIRATION & INSTANT GRATIFICATION

We often think that when we get an idea, we must take immediate action on it. This isn't always necessary, and how you flow around this depends on your personality. I recommend taking note of the inspiration but not necessarily immediately acting on it. I keep a gigantic Google Doc list of all the inspiration that comes in. There are hundreds of ideas in there. Blog post topics, newsletter ideas, sales emails, offer ideas, course ideas, and book ideas.

I'll look to this list when I feel stale or notice I'm rinsing and repeating more than usual in my daily work. And then, I make a plan to take action on something on the list.

When you can't seem to find your next idea, it doesn't mean it isn't there, though that's what it feels like. We know there's a difference between feeling full of ideas and empty, yet many creatives blame the infamous writer's block when they can't seem to get any words out, thinking the inspiration well has run dry.

What if I told you that there's nothing in the way of writing inspiration?

Instead, what if you're just out of lived experiences to share? I know how easy it is for me to settle into writing from my home office and only venture outside the house for essentials. If we're living in a state of constant consumption and not experiencing, it won't fill us up and we'll have nothing to write about. Ask yourself: what do you need to see, hear, do, know, or feel before you have more to share?

Or are you getting too much inspiration and don't know where to start? Here's an example: I'd had an idea about how to structure a copywriting course (intuitive inspiration), and that idea was tugging at me right before I started writing this book. This could have pulled me away from the book-writing process (intuitive creation). Instead, I planned for future action-taking. Before I began writing the book, I quickly outlined the course, drafted a sales page, and planned to do a small launch for the people I'd already been working with, as well as my newsletter subscribers. Discerning the difference between divine guidance and distraction takes practice.

I put dates on the calendar for when I'd take action and planned to deliver the course a few months after creating the outline — and drafting this book.

Now, having a few projects on the go can be a great way to keep all of them feeling shiny and newish. At this moment in time, I have two other books in the works. I work on them sporadically and keep track of new inspiration or ideas — but I'm not in there as diligently or consistently as I am with this one, writing each day as the first activity at my computer.

Make sure you have a place to capture all the inspiration that comes in. Keep a notebook on you, and a few throughout your home, and use your voice notes on your phone. Just make sure to plan time to take all the ideas you've captured in various places and centralize them somewhere. My ideas are centralized in a Google Doc.

CHAPTER 13
INTUITIVE PLANNING

Intuitive Inspiration
Intuitive Planning
Intuitive Creation
Intuitive Editing & Refining

I'm a pantser — flying by the seat of my pants — so I feel you if you're also one who hesitates to make plans. I resisted plans for much of my life, preferring to jump in and do what was right in front of me. Whatever comes next, the next step that needs to be taken to get to the next, and the next. I would say things like, "My plans never work anyway."

Now, instead, I like to create an intuitive plan. This is a loose plan that I know will likely change. I've tried forcing. It's what prompted that break from writing I took a few years ago. I learned pretty quickly that forcing is exhausting — and in my experience, delivers shitty results. When I sense I'm pushing too hard, I choose surrender. If you're surrendered, you can't help but go with the flow.

Now when life gets bonkers and shit hits the fan, I'm always grateful that I have a strategy to fall back on. The plan is there to catch you when life throws you around — because it will. Yes, your plan can change.

Way back when I said my plans didn't work, that wasn't true. The truth was I wasn't following my plan. How do you know if a plan doesn't work for you if you never follow it through to the end?

Planning is a great activity to do in the spring rhythm — whether that's your personal spring, when the tulips are popping out of the ground, or when the moon is in the waxing phase. More on this in Chapter 16.

This section on planning goes deep. Take your time with this section. It's the biggest, and arguably, the most important to lay a foundation for the rest of the writing process.

The intuitive approach to planning is to look ahead to the whole year and loosely plan all your writing projects. Once I have a rough outline for the year, I recommend quarterly planning for more specific details. A year is too much time and makes it too easy to slip into thinking we have more time than we do, and a month isn't enough. Planning your whole year at once makes it too convenient to push tasks to later on — only to never get to them. Twelve weeks is both long enough to see results and short enough to drive massive action.

Use the plan as a creative container. Create within the container as it works for you and your life.

If the events following 2020 taught us anything, it's that even the best plan can go out the window. For instance, I had a loose writing plan that year. Which I tossed out the window that March when I pivoted to help people write what they needed — this happened to be crisis copy and new websites to get businesses off the ground in lightning speed. Instead of a new plan for the year, I planned in smaller chunks. I still had my targets set on my big writing projects — and I allowed more flexibility in all my writing.

Each month, quarter, and year, I review my body of writing work and then look ahead to what I'll create next.

I could get into the weeds here and talk about how time is an illusion and doesn't exist, but for the purpose of this book that lives in the 3D world, let's make some grounded plans. Maybe my next book is about being a 12D writer. Hmmm.

To help you decide what to write next, it can help to look back.

Step 1. Look back and celebrate

One month at a time, review your published writing. Consider gathering:

- Stats: Which blog posts, podcasts, social posts, or articles had the most engagement, views, comments? If you have time, consider tracking this information in a spreadsheet with relevant stats and links.
- What months did your writing flow?
- What topics resonated most with readers?
- Which felt easy to write?
- What topics could you write five more pieces about?
- Could any of your blog posts later be used in a book? As a free download? Turned into a workshop (free or paid)?
- If your writing naturally falls into categories or buckets, which categories were the most fun to write about? Which ones felt like a slog?
- Write three to five things that worked well for your writing process. Did batch writing help? Did focusing on certain topics help? Did writing at a

particular time of day and day of the week make it feel easier?

- Remember to celebrate! First, look at how much you created and put out in the world. This is a great starting point!

Intuitive Writing Tip

Celebrate every writing win! When you celebrate, you release feel-good chemicals in your brain, helping you want to naturally keep going.

Step 2. Decide your purpose

- What format do you enjoy? Blogging, podcasting, emailing? A combination?
- What's your purpose for creating content? Growing your audience? Establishing your expertise? Getting more eyeballs on your website and offers (SEO)? All of these?
- Are you writing about topics your ideal audience wants to read?
- Are there things you enjoy writing about more than others?

Step 3. Set your intentions

- Did you choose a word of the year? Or a few words? Or a feeling?
- What are one to three of your big business or writing goals for the year? The quarter?
- Fast forward to the end of the quarter or year — what do you want to say about that time?

- Whatever you choose — you can refine as you move throughout the year. Write it on a sticky note, write the word at the front of your planner, or design a desktop wallpaper.

Step 4. Look at the year / quarter / month ahead

- Print out monthly pages, use your paper planner, a Google Doc or spreadsheet

Step 5. Schedule blank space first

- Review your personal schedule, time off, hectic times of the year at home, busy times in your business, holidays.
- How much time do you want to take off? Block those times first. You can always open it back up later.

Step 6. Plan your business sales cycles

- Your promotion schedule, launches, upcoming offers — plot these on your calendar and then work backward in your content leading up to your offers or sales cycles.
- Make sure you're answering the question: what does my ideal client need to know or believe to sign up or work with me?
- Mark holidays and theme months so you can write relevant content.
- Review the moon cycle (you can add it to your Google calendar): Click "Other calendars," then "Browse calendars of interest" and select the

calendars to add to yours (Moon is at the bottom). See why you'd want to do this in Chapter 16.

- Note busy and slower months – you could dedicate these for focused writing time, or consider a promotion in your business.
- Once you decide what you'll promote, rearrange your sales schedule to fit your personal schedule and any other relevant times.

Step 7. Brainstorm your main themes

Consider all your content like a charcuterie board. Each of your blog posts is inspiring and helpful on its own. When enjoyed one after another with a small taste from all the other accompanying content, the experience is even better.

This is why organizing your content into buckets or a few key themes will help your work appear as a charcuterie board. You wouldn't drop an oatmeal cookie, spaghetti, or okra on your board. It wouldn't fit.

Typically, one to five themes or topics will naturally emerge.

Scan your existing content. If you had to put this work into categories, where would they naturally fit? Then, consider your list of groups and think about combining or removing some if there are too many. And if you notice you have a single theme, that's great too.

You can absolutely stick to one subject or add more if you feel inspired.

- Think about what you want to be known for. Do you help people with a specific challenge? How do you want people to remember you? Do you want them to remember you for your ability to take a personal story and apply a business lesson? Do you want to be known for your straight, no-BS talk?

- Consider what you could talk about all day. When you talk about something, and it brings you energy, life, and light, that right there is content *gold.* List out all the topics that make you feel giddy with excitement. Subjects so good to talk about that you simply have to get them out. When you write about what lights your fire, you'll feel good. When you feel good, your readers feel good, and isn't this the whole dang point?
- What do people always ask for your advice on as it relates to your business?
- When you notice you're giving the same advice to different people and it's something you can help your audience with, offering that is service. And when you serve your audience, they appreciate it.
- What does your ideal client need to know or understand before they buy? Back into this by filling in the blanks of what people need to know and believe before they'll sign up for each step along your customer journey. *For my reader to want to sign up, they need to first believe______. People need to understand ______ before they want ______.*
- Now, write out your list of possible themes — maybe you have one, three, or even six. Review each topic on the list. Do you enjoy and want to continue talking about these topics? If not, go ahead and strike some. And if you do love these topics, now you have some boundaries to help you with your brainstorming. Having boundaries for your brainstorming and creative projects will help you create. While many assume that creative people

need wide-open spaces in which to write, I can tell you from working with many kinds of makers and being creative myself that without a container to create in, I spin in circles, or I do nothing.

Intuitive Writing Tip
What feels good to create feels good for your readers to read.

Step 8. Make a topic inspiration list

- List-makers rejoice! Now, you're going to compile a big list. There are over one hundred topic ideas on my content list. I look to this list as a menu of things I can potentially write about — *not* as a to-do list.
- Revisit any existing lists of topics you have from the previous period — are there any topics you want to tackle next?
- Review your previous year or quarter's content highlights — what topics do you want to rewrite, update, or explore more deeply?
- Look outside your industry for fresh inspiration. If you're in the food industry you could look to sports, the auto industry, or fashion.

Step 9. Create a twelve-week plan

Next, make your content plan fit into your life and business.

Starting with a blank page, list your personal and business values at the top of the page. (Mine are health and healing, family, and business.) These will be your north star for everything you create.

Then, list your one to three writing goals for the coming quarter.

Create a specific list of things you'll do each week for the three main areas of your life. A caveat: some of this will look like lifestyle advice. This is by design as we can't look at our writing life without looking at our whole lives. Now, there are a lot of tasks you can do to accomplish each goal. Before deciding what goes on the plan, brainstorm a list and choose the tasks that are either proven to generate the results you want or add some new ones that you want to experiment with.

If I have three writing goals for the quarter, they might look like this:

1. Draft book
2. Launch new offer
3. Publish a weekly blog

Then I'll set up my personal life to support that. Here's a peek at one of my sample weeks.

Week 1, January 1

Health and Healing:

- Yoga 2x
- Weights 2x
- Morning pages 5x
- Read 1 chapter a day

Personal and Family:

- Phone away at 7 p.m.
- Social media–free day

- Date night
- Practice learning from book chapter

Business:

- SFD of 2 blog posts
- Outline sales page for new offer
- Write 2 book chapters

Intuitive Writing Tip

If you need to change your writing plan, it's okay! A plan is there to guide you.

We're all constantly changing. A plan is there to support you and make your life easier, not harder. It's there to guide you when you need it — not shove you into a too-tight, too-small, constrictive box.

Keep creating, keep writing, and keep going. Build that body of work!

As you create, keep in mind that the more you tap into your creativity, the more you'll discover. I promise you'll unlock more possibilities than you could ever imagine.

You can download a twelve-week planning template in the resources.

Step 10. Block time on your calendar for strategic tasks

Once you have your tasks, make the time on your calendar and honor it. You might block sixty minutes a day for lunch and an hour each day to make progress on your strategic business tasks. You might block Mondays and Fridays for working on your business.

- Based on your schedule, sales planning, and themes in your business, start plotting specific topics to happen in certain weeks or months, depending on your publishing frequency.
- You can plot on your Google calendar, in a spreadsheet, in your paper planner, or with pen and paper.

Know that the plan is there to guide you. You have full control to reorder any topics as you see fit.

Step 11. Work your twelve-week plan

Print your twelve-week plan and move the weekly to-dos to your daily tasks before diving into work each morning. New things will pop up — keep what you can, delegate, move some items around, or remove them.

Revisit the plan at the start and end of each week and each day. See what needs to move around and what tasks keep slipping.

If a writing task keeps dropping off your plan, investigate why. Is it that this task isn't aligned right now? Could you be avoiding it for some reason that you can address?

For any tasks you remove from your plan, I suggest putting them in a "parking lot" section at the bottom of your twelve-week plan and then reviewing whether you'll include them in your next quarterly writing plan.

I've been planning this way for a while now and continue to refine my process. I encourage you to do the same.

Sometimes, I'll spend more time than I should serving others instead of making sure my tasks happen first. This causes them to slide off my weekly plan, only to end up moving them to the following week. If I didn't have the plan in place, I wouldn't know this — it keeps me aware of where I can focus better.

DOES YOUR PLAN EXCITE YOU?

Your plan should feel exciting and make you a little uneasy. After all, you're stretching yourself to reach new goals and do things in a new way. If your plan is filled with things you're already doing all the time, give it another look. When you're excited about your plan and start seeing evidence that the actions you're taking align with the goals you're going after, it feels good — which begets more good feelings about your plan. Which also means you're more likely to follow it.

Intuitive Writing Tip
Create a plan for writing that pushes you out of your comfort zone and feels exciting.

Planning my life, business, and writing in this way feels authentic and aligned, and it gets me fired up to create. I hope you find the plan does this for you too. Maybe you've already changed your perspective on planning.

CHAPTER 14
INTUITIVE CREATION

Intuitive Inspiration
Intuitive Planning
Intuitive Creation
Intuitive Editing & Refining

Yes! Action time! This stage is exciting because it's where we see the most momentum — there's so much energy in this phase.

To pace yourself, it's great to take a small action regularly, instead of massive action all at once. That said, do what works for you and if you're feeling the fire, by all means: Go!

I've seen that small actions over time add up and are much more manageable long-term. This is the difference between writing a book or a website in forty-eight hours or spacing it out over a month or two or ten.

When you're taking action, optimally, you'll already have a plan for writing and editing and approach each phase one at a time.

Some examples of small actions you can take to prepare you for writing:

- Blocking time to write on days you know you'll have quiet time
- Journaling during new moons and full moons
- Finding an accountability partner
- Arranging your writing space
- Joining a writing community

This is where you walk over to the faucet, turn the knob, and let the words flow. This is the messiest part of the whole process. Creation is a beautiful, messy thing — just like how we got here.

Hopefully, you have a bucket to catch the water first. A bucket can be your boundary — your thirty-day or twelve-week writing plan, a word count goal, a forty-five-minute calendar block, several paragraphs to fill on your website, twenty-five minutes on a Pomodoro timer, or a target page count.

When you're approaching your first creation, the words coming out of your fingertips may hardly make sense. Keep going. Creation is a process of finding flow. Go back to Chapter 2 if you need to revisit the idea of the SFD. When you've done all the planning to prepare for creation, the flow comes more naturally and easily.

Also, remember that you're constantly changing; each creation session may feel different. Some are more challenging than others. That's okay. When I was writing this book during NaNoWriMo (more on this in Chapter 21), I had days when it felt like I was searching for the right words in molasses and had to use both hands to pull them out.

But here's the thing: Keep looking forward when you're in the process of creation. If I spend too much energy looking back, I'll see nonsensical words, more red pen marks than I saw in tenth-grade English class, and an overwhelming mess.

It's easy to let the mind run wild during this tangled

holiday lights phase. I hear the thoughts creeping in: *Oh, this is such a mess, how will I ever clean it up?* You get started the same way you'd clean up after dropping a Costco-sized jar of strawberry jam on white tile (true story). Hovering above the mess, you want to cry, run away, or leave it for another day. But you know that mess needs to be dealt with. As you start cleaning it up, bit by bit, tile by tile, it gets easier.

Sometimes when the cat pukes on the rug, I leave it to harden so it'll be easier to clean up. That's what creation is like: a cat's hairball in the middle of the living room. Puke that creation up and let it sit for a week before you go to clean it up. Giving it extra time will make it easier to clean up later.

That's what editing is like.

CHAPTER 15
INTUITIVE EDITING & REFINING

Intuitive Inspiration
Intuitive Planning
Intuitive Creation
Intuitive Editing & Refining

When I started writing *Unfussy Life,* I thought writing would be the most challenging phase. I was wrong. Editing was much harder because there was a lot of rewriting, moving around, tweaking, and removing during the editing process.

Editing requires a very special balance of maintaining a ten-thousand-foot view as you travel along the foggy ground. Being so close to the material makes it hard to see through the fog. So, depending on where you're at in your writing process, this might be a good time to bring in outside reinforcements.

For your website, blog, or book there are editors to help you take the word vomit and clean it up. When it comes to books, especially, editors are just as important as the author writing the work.

An editor sees the beauty that's trying to come out through a pile of words. They're in tune. They're often following their guts and intuitively tweaking and editing a piece of work when they don't really even realize why they're suggesting a change or moving something around.

It can be helpful to look at editing as an activity with distinct qualities. While writing takes letting go, surrendering, and allowing the words to fall out, editing is the moving and working with those words, like a sculptor modeling a piece of clay. Before touching the clay, it needs time to rest a bit — but not so long that it turns to stone.

Michelangelo sculpted *David*, and this was after a bunch of other sculptors attempted the same subject but couldn't do it. Michelangelo, however, said he saw David in the marble. All he did was let the figure emerge. You can look at your piece of writing like this too. You have a sense of what you want the work to be. You can "see" it. It's your job to sculpt it so that it comes through as clearly as possible.

When you've taken it as far as you can and don't know what to do next — this is where a professional can come in and help you see the next step.

Hiring a professional editor is pure gold. They'll sense what you're trying to say and help you make it clear. Also, someone who plays with words for lots of writers in a variety of genres brings a wealth of knowledge and experience to your project.

If you're confident in editing your own work — go for it. That said, at the very least, I suggest hiring a proofreader to make sure there are no typos in your book.

When it comes to blog posts, email newsletters, and most of my website copy — I edit them myself. For this work, where typos and some grammar mistakes are not the end of the world, I edit myself, but I allow some space and time between the writing and the editing.

When editing a blog post, setting it aside during lunch, or

even for a week or two, will help make the editing process go more smoothly. For a book, setting it aside for a few weeks, at least, is helpful.

When writing this chapter, I let it sit for at least a month between the SFD and my first round of edits.

You'll find specific editing tips later, in Chapter 25.

JOURNAL PROMPTS

1. As you think about the work you've created in the past, what phase feels easiest to you?
2. What phase do you find yourself getting stuck in? How could you plan for getting stuck next time so you can easily move through it?
3. Which phase are most of your projects in?

CHAPTER 16
WRITING WITH NATURE'S RHYTHMS

It wasn't until my late thirties that I learned about tuning into my menstrual cycle to help me go with the flow in life. Up until then, I knew I'd have a period each month, I'd ovulate sometime in between, and that was the time to get pregnant (or avoid pregnancy). Other than that, I never paid much attention. It was simply something that was always there, never asking for too much or needing anything from me. I've never experienced massive mood swings (though my husband might tell you differently) or cramps, and I viewed it as a part of life. Not really an inconvenience or anything like the way the media talks about it. It was just — there, like a patio paver.

A few years ago, someone in my writing community shared what she was learning about nature's rhythms and how she could apply them to her business.

I'm going to tell you about these rhythms — the seasons, the moon, and the menstrual cycle. I promise it will help your writing practice. Know that when I first heard this information, all I did was let it sink in. I didn't take any specific action on it. Instead, I continued to read about it and started paying attention. I didn't change how I did anything, but merely tuned in and noticed what was going on. I did that for a few months and then slowly started to plan my writing activities around nature.

If you're judging this as some airy-fairy bullshit or think it doesn't apply to you — stop. First, you're literally here reading this because of nature's cycle — your mother ovulated (which carries similar energy to the full moon and summer), and your father contributed sperm. Second, if you think paying attention to nature is, well, unnatural, then you can carry on with forcing things and pushing to the brink of burnout. And third, even if you no longer have your cycle or never had one to begin with, you're still part of nature's rhythms.

Now, why do we want to write with nature's rhythms? Because when we know what's going on with our bodies and the planets, including the one we live on, it makes everything we're doing easier.

I now track my cycle on a Google calendar and schedule my work accordingly throughout the year.

I've applied what I learned about my cycle to my writing practice — helping me write and publish more in less time while looking after my body first. The results? I'm calmer, more confident, and feeling more magnetic, productive and creative than ever. You're seeing the proof that it works — I followed the advice you see on these pages to bring this very book to you.

Intuitive writing is all about using the moon and/or your cycle to align your intentions to your action and inaction. The good news is that she (the moon) is consistent and reliable, so if you don't have a menstrual cycle, look to the moon.

Let's back up to get to know the sun:

- Has a predictable twenty-four-hour cycle

- Is considered the masculine — carrying similar energetic qualities as men, who have a relatively consistent twenty-four-hour hormone cycle

Next, let's get to know the moon:

- Has a predictable cycle lasting about 29.5 days
- Has four distinct energetic phases
- These phases and energies have the same energetic quality as the four phases of the menstrual cycle and the four seasons

If you have a menstrual cycle, here are the phases and approximate lengths:

- Menstrual phase (From day 1 to 5)
- Follicular phase (From day 6 to 10)
- Ovulation phase (From day 11 to 16)
- Luteal phase (From day 17 to 28)

Here's how the moon phases line up with the seasons and a menstrual cycle:

- New moon / winter / menstrual phase
- Waxing moon / spring / follicular phase
- Full moon / summer / ovulation
- Waning moon / fall / luteal phase

Both masculine and feminine qualities are woven into each phase of writing. Writing is surrendering and letting go (feminine), and also taking action (masculine). Editing is also letting go (feminine), and action-taking (masculine), doing the work to refine and carve out the work.

Let's further explore the qualities of each cycle and how you can align your writing with these phases. If you have a menstrual cycle, look to this first, and then the moon.

NEW MOON / WINTER / MENSTRUAL PHASE

I drafted this chapter on a new moon in Scorpio, in the fall season, and my follicular phase. A mixed bag of energy. I started this book project for NaNoWriMo on day six of my cycle — spring energy to get me going.

The new moon is a time to go within. It's a time to plant seeds in the dark soil that you'll later reap.

There's some science around the brain's right and left hemispheres being closer together when you're menstruating, making you more intuitive at this time. Because there's barely any light reflected in the sky from the moon, you look inward for that light instead. So this is a great time to make decisions. If I have a big decision to make, I'll sleep on it, bleed on it, or ask myself during a new moon. I need time, rest, and the space to go within before knowing what I'll do about something.

Here are some intuitive-writing ways to play with the new moon / winter / menstrual phase:

- Write intentions on the new moon for your writing project. These should be less like a list of ego wants for Santa Claus, and worded more like "May God show me . . ." or "I intend . . ."
- Dedicate time to journaling on your writing project without taking any specific action.
- Try future-state journaling and write about what your writing project does for you and others as if it's already finished.

- Get quiet, meditate, take a bath, walk in nature, and tune into your intuition for how you receive messages. How do they come to you?
- Make decisions about what writing project to focus on, start in the spring, or finish in the fall.
- Since there's not a lot of light in the night sky, you may be more tired than usual — this usually isn't the time to push. If you rest now, you'll have more energy for all the writing and editing things later. Block your calendar for a day or two or create as much spaciousness as you can.

WAXING MOON / SPRING / FOLLICULAR PHASE

The energy of spring has a fresh green sprouting quality to it. Those seeds you planted in the dark are beginning to germinate and sprout. They may be starting to emerge now.

This is a time for brainstorming those brilliant ideas. Have a ton of ideas swirling around in your mind? This is a great time to jot them down. You'll naturally have more ideas right now. You may have some clever ones that surprise you too.

If you feel overwhelmed by looking at all these ideas, know that you don't need to take action on any of them yet. You've done your job by capturing them and will come back to one when the time is right.

Intuitive-writing ways to play with the waxing moon / spring / follicular phase:

- Make plans for those intentions you planted at the new moon, adding key dates to your calendar.
- Decide which actions you'll start taking on your writing projects.

- You might notice you have a ton of new ideas in this phase — keep a document or journal nearby to capture them. Trust that the idea will be there for you when you're ready; there's no need to shift your focus to a shiny new project.
- Start taking action with some SFD writing. You might write a little on a bunch of topics, or write a lot (remember, no editing yet) on a big project.

FULL MOON / SUMMER / OVULATION PHASE

Consider this time the climax, the culmination, the full spotlight — the plants are bursting with beauty and are radiating in their full vibrance.

Think of this as visibility time. Maybe this is when you'll share your work with the world. Plan your book release party or website launch around this date. If you run an online business where you launch a few times a year, this can be a great time to close your shopping carts.

The extra light in the sky is a free jumbo spotlight shining a light on whatever you need to pay attention to — so that you can let something go.

Intuitive-writing ways to play with the full moon / summer / ovulation phase:

- You might have the most energy right now — plan a longer writing session, writing retreat, or some batching sessions. (See the batching section in Chapter 21.) Share your work with trusted readers or friends or even the world because you're at your most magnetic during this phase.
- The moon is shining a ton of light right now — what do you want to shine a light on?

- Consider what's being illuminated for you right now so that you can let go of it. Is it time to dissolve an old idea that feels stale? What wants to go? Let what wants to go fall away so that you can make space for what wants to come.
- Write down all the old beliefs you have about writing that are no longer serving you and burn them.

WANING MOON / FALL / LUTEAL PHASE

Think pumpkin spice, changing leaves, and harvest. All those seeds you planted in the dark are ready to reap.

Think about a squirrel running around getting ready for winter — picking, gathering, and nesting.

Intuitive-writing ways to play with the waning moon / fall / luteal phase:

- NaNoWriMo happens during this time in the northern hemisphere — harvest those words that have been marinating all year — they're ripe and ready. Pull that carrot, turnip, and sweet potato out of the ground (writing) and make a delicious savory soup with it (editing).
- If it's cold where you live during fall, you might naturally be indoors more — using that inside time to do the writing work you so love.
- This is an excellent phase for editing. I intentionally planned a few rounds of revisions on my books during my luteal phase and during waning moons because it's a time when I'm naturally paying more attention to detail — I

caught a bunch of minor typos and errors that I had missed so many times before!
- As we're getting ready to go inward for the new moon, we might have less energy. Having a flexible schedule during this phase will be a gift.

Here's an example of what my life looks like in a given month (or *moonth*) moving through the four phases.

1. New Moon

- Blocking my calendar, making sure there's time for journaling, intuitive downloads, making decisions, and feeling into what I want to create in the next moon cycle.
- Rest, extra comforting and grounding foods like potatoes and beets, lots of stretching, yoga, and walking.

2. Waxing Moon

- Planning, brainstorming, scheduling meetings, gathering ideas, taking action, launching a new book or program, and writing SFDs of book chapters, website copy, or blog posts.
- More movement, additional gym sessions, lots of spring-like foods such as asparagus and spinach.

3. Full Moon

- Doing podcast interviews, recording course materials, scheduling the height of a launch, delivering talks and workshops, pitching.

- Full energy, lifting heavy weights, lots of action, visibility, and risk-taking. Enjoying bright foods like dragon fruit and berries.

4. Waning Moon

- Editing and refining blog posts, book chapters, and website copy. Revisiting and refreshing old blog posts; finalizing, completing, and reviewing all the tiny details like chapter references in a book.
- Moving a little slower, more yoga, less intensity at the gym and eating foods that feel like fall — sweet potatoes, chickpeas, cabbage.

It's important to note that there's no judgment here. You know those days when the life-affirming words just fell out of your fingers like acorns from an oak tree in autumn or raindrops during a storm? And then, a week later, you're sitting at the page ready to burn your entire project to the ground and maybe shut down your business?

That's because you've changed, the weather has changed, your hormones have changed, and the moon has changed. Literally, the entire universe is different from minute to minute and week to week, so naturally, every writing and editing session will feel different.

Once we know this, we can easily move forward and stop wasting time feeling annoyed and resentful. And even looking back at our past prolific selves and feeling jealousy — who was that word-slinging wonder? It was you. It was a piece of you. That version of you is still in there. It's not lost. it just needs something different from you now.

I'm only scratching the surface of following nature's

rhythms. There are entire books written on these subjects. Find some listed in the resources if you want to go deeper.

Also, the other planets are always influencing us here on earth. You can find a great, modern astrologer to help you decode what's going on in the cosmos and how it relates to your life.

If this is the first time you've heard about writing with nature's rhythms, I suggest that the only action you take for a few months is to simply notice what's going on. After taking some time to pay attention, experiment with planning a single writing project to line up with your cycle or the moon's for the coming month. Stay curious and open to see what happens.

Now, a head's up — what I see some people do is blame nature for why they're not writing. "I'm just so full of inspiration during this waxing moon that I can't get to the page" or "It's the waning moon and I hate the world so I can't edit my blog posts right now." The moon, the weather, and your body are never to blame. When you hear yourself saying why you can't do something and follow it up with "because," I guarantee what comes next is an *excuse*.

You can be an intuitive writer who makes no excuses. At the end of the day, it's you who's accountable.

JOURNAL PROMPTS

1. Note what's going on in your cycle if you have one, what's going on with the moon and the weather outside today. Notice how you're feeling and what you've been writing. How does it feel?
2. At the beginning of each season or moon cycle, consider what you want to do this season — what's calling to you to create?

3. Reading back over the seasons and moon phases, what phase(s) feel best for you to brainstorm, write, edit? Can you think of specific projects where you intuitively worked within a supportive, energetic container?
4. As you write morning pages each day, consider exploring what's going on in nature.
5. Keep a daily log in a dedicated notebook to capture what's going on with you, the moon, and the weather outside.

CHAPTER 17
WRITING WITHOUT EGO

As I mentioned, my goal in writing this book was to create the entire thing following my own advice, which means keeping ego's sneaky fingers out of here.

This question of writing without ego has been rolling around in my mind for years. Now, only time will tell how successful I was at this endeavor — time has a way of showing us where we have more work to do.

To look at ego, we're going to go back to the unconscious mind. My NLP coach says that we marry our unconscious minds — so when my husband does something that irritates me, it's only showing me something that I need to look at within myself.

One morning a few years ago (before I unsubscribed him from my email newsletter list), he said, "Nice article."

"Thanks, babe!" (It's always nice to know someone is reading, even if it's while on the toilet.)

"Too bad it's not really you," he quipped flatly.

Wait. What?

Mind you, this wasn't the first time we'd had this discussion. He has pointed out more than once that the version of me who shows up in my writing isn't the version of me he sees at home.

As someone who makes an effort to show up fully and authentically, his commentary gave me pause.

For a long time, he was, in fact, correct.

As a copywriter, I often slip into a persona. I spend a lot of time and energy getting into my client's heads and *their* client's heads so that I can sound like them.

In my own writing, I write the SFD without thinking. Turning my brain off and letting the words out. Then, when editing, I choose my words carefully and aim to be impeccable, honest, direct, and supportive in my speech. I sometimes stop to ask myself, "Is this really me talking?" "Am I performing?" "Am I trying to control what the reader thinks of me so that they'll like me?"

Enter the ego — inserting thoughts where previously I was writing from the heart.

How do I know when it's really me on the page? How do I know if I'm writing from a place of surrender or writing to convince, please, or to influence a specific outcome?

This takes us back to the idea of writing "drunk" — that uninhibited place where we let ourselves go in the SFD. The writing needs to land safely in some kind of container.

So if we drop ego and write drunk, who's speaking then? Is it really us or is it our muse?

Creatives often talk about the muse as a mysterious, unpredictable visitor. Like it's an external-to-us creature that sweeps in, shows us what to write and then flies away. But really, could the muse be our unconscious minds? Or God, Jesus, the Divine, or our higher selves taking the wheel (er . . . keyboard) to share what needs to be written.

What I do know is that when we're controlling, it's ego.

When we're surrendering, it's us (or a higher power speaking through us).

Now, the ego isn't "bad" — it serves a purpose. Just like every organ we came into this world with, our ego is a part of us. The problem is that with a lot of us, the ego is trying to steal the show.

How does ego show up in our writing? In a completely unscientific way, I've noticed that the articles I spend the least amount of time thinking about, just pouring out in a kind of meditative state, are the ones that people email me most often about. They thank me for writing it or simply say, "Oh, I love this!"

That's the same approach I took with this book. I wrote it so fast, focusing only on what I wanted to say and thinking less about what it was supposed to be or was trying to be. It didn't need to *be* anything. It just needed to come out. Surrender to the writing process; let go of the outcome.

To write from this surrendered place, managing my state to ensure I was writing from a calm, relaxed place was key. You can revisit state management in Chapter 8.

So, is the key to getting ego out of our writing just *not* thinking and turning off our brains?

These are all questions I asked myself as I peeled back the layers. We're all changing and evolving. As a writer, and in this book, I'm going to contradict myself as I dig deeper. My opinions will change. When *Unfussy Life* was finally ready to be out in the world, there was so much in there that I'd written that I wanted to revise — my ideas weren't exactly as I felt; I was eating plant-based again and I was doing so much more healing and ego eradication work. But still, I let that book out into the world and let it be what it wanted to be — detaching from the outcome.

And that's how I know I'm stretching and doing the work.

Letting go of ego isn't pleasant. Maybe you've heard about folks who use plant medicine like ayahuasca to obliterate the ego. Ayahuasca is a South American psychoactive mixed drink people often travel to the Amazon to use as a ceremonial, spiritual medicine. It releases N,N-Dimethyltryptamine, or "DMT" — the same chemical that is released in your brain when you die. As you journey with this plant, you're essentially "dying"; your ego is dying, and there's nothing you can do. It's intense (so I hear — I won't be trying it because it's become too mainstream and can cause a lot of damage).

I've always been doing some form of healing and self-improvement, but early in 2021, I dialed it up several notches (no DMT was involved) and had some other big realizations about ego.

We can only write without ego if we're living without ego. At the time I'm writing this, I'm so aware of my ego and all the ways it's attempting (and sometimes succeeding) to run the show, and yet I'm still trying to drop it all and show up to the page.

I write from the heart, saying what I want to say without much of a filter. I don't try to control other people's perceptions of me and my work. I just aim to put the best damn piece of work out there every time.

I go within and express myself from there.

When I notice I'm overthinking something (like this chapter, for instance), I get stuck. But when I look away from the computer screen and surrender, I let the words that want to come through fall onto the page.

As you tune into your intuition, you'll get closer to many gifts. Some of mine are helping business owners see what they need to write, bringing writers together, and bringing creatives to the table so that they can create. It's not *me* who makes this happen. It's how I tune into the Divine and allow the guidance to work through me. I'm a channel for this work. It's not mine. My name is on the cover only because I'm the vessel that brought it here into the 3D world.

To obliterate ego in our writing, we need to do deep healing work. Here are some ways you can get started by looking at your writing.

1. Writing like no one will read it.

Writing is a powerful tool for figuring shit out. If writing it helped you make sense of a situation, you'll be okay. Trust the process and move on — and keep writing.

2. Try freewriting or stream-of-consciousness writing.

Morning pages (I told you they'd come up a lot) are also a tool to move the ego out of the way so we can write from a clear place. When we're letting the words fall out without forcing, thinking, or controlling, something else takes over. Let yourself co-create with the Divine. When I read back over most of my writing, I don't consciously remember writing most of it. *Who wrote that? It's pretty fucking good! Oh, that was me!* When I write from a meditative state, with eyes closed, I know I'm only a channel for what wants to come through. My job is only to surrender and get the words out on the page — not to control or force, but just to let the words out.

3. Edit just enough for clarity and readability.

As a writer, I know that what I often set out to write sometimes looks totally different from the finished product. If this book read like a journal, you'd have a hard time reading it. Editing is the process that turns my half-coherent rambling into something you can easily understand.

Intuitive Writing Tip

Writing without ego means being fully present and surrendered. We can only do this if we're actively doing the work – the work to heal our wounds, look inward, see where we can unplug from the matrix, and begin looking at life and our surroundings as an interaction and less as an integration.

CHAPTER 18
FINDING FEEL-GOOD FLOW IN YOUR WRITING PRACTICE

When we're in the flow, ego can't be running the show.

Finding flow.

Get in the flow.

Create in the flow.

Flowing.

I'm in the flow.

What the hell does this mean?

Flow state, according to Wikipedia: "In positive psychology, a flow state, also known colloquially as being in the zone, is the mental state in which a person performing some activity is fully immersed in a feeling of energized focus, full involvement, and enjoyment in the process of the activity."

Flow is feminine — circular, round, moves like water — but I realize it runs much deeper than that as I explore the concept further.

You've likely felt flow many times in your life — maybe you've just never given it a name. Flow is where I want to write from. It's where I brainstorm, create, and refine, and even where I cook, coach, and paint on a canvas from. For me, these are all creative activities when I lose track of time.

Flow is a meditative state where I feel like I don't have a body anymore. I'm so intensely immersed in what I'm doing that the rest of the world doesn't exist. Flow is what's going on when time seems to stop. Flow happens when you're leaning into discomfort and learning something challenging.

Athletes get into flow when they're playing their sport — and really, it's inspiring to watch. I've also seen it in my kids — my son when he's in the net on the hockey rink, stopping pucks flying at frightening speeds. And my daughter when surrounded by piles of paint or jewelry-making supplies or when she's cantering a horse around the arena. Nothing else matters but that moment.

Watching my kids get lost in Legos, painting, or learning a new song on the piano, I see them living and breathing in a flow state. Or when I watch my dogs roll around in the grass, I see four-legged beings completely grounded in flow — not a care in the world.

Flow feels fucking good, so we want to be there, but chasing it doesn't work. It's about surrendering and allowing.

Intuitive Writing Tip

Find flow outside of your writing practice. The exciting part is that how we achieve flow state isn't necessarily as important, only that we experience the state as often as possible. See where you flow in cooking, sports, art, whatever you like!

Think back to early 2020 (I know, we're going there a lot . . . just hear me out). If the way you found flow was working in a café, traveling, or connecting with friends over dinner, and it was suddenly more challenging — what happened?

If you didn't find a way to replace the flow state, this could have made the feelings of isolation, anger, and sadness feel even stronger. This is not to minimize negative states, but if your way of finding flow came to a grinding halt in 2020, finding a fresh method to access the flow state became urgent.

More than just feeling good, though, flow has a purpose. It makes you a better person, listener, and creator. Flow doesn't always look light and airy. There are also many moments when we're embracing the discomfort of writing something new. And in those moments of breaching our comfort zone, we find flow.

It goes like this:

I suck.

I suck.

This is hard.

I'll keep going.

I suck.

I'm kinda good at this.

I'm good.

Where'd the time go?

This is fun!

I feel so satisfied.

When can I do this again?

Think about flow in your writing practice. When you didn't want to write something, maybe even resented that you had to do it at all, and forced the words out of you, how did that feel? And more importantly, how did your reader or potential client receive it on the other end?

I've also found it exciting that flow state can apply to groups. When my writing community gathers on Zoom and we're in the zone of creating, some people call it magic — the ideas that came through, the progress they made, or even the breakthroughs they had in their writing work. When we get together in community and find flow, we're increasing the collective energy — our energetic signatures merge and we can suddenly access a more vibrant energy level than we could have imagined — handy when your enthusiasm isn't there. During our two-hour co-writing sessions in The Intuitive Writing School Community, I check in with everyone at the halfway point. I'm careful to speak softly during check-ins because many people are so in the flow that they're startled when I start speaking.

And even when business owners feel stuck on a name for their new offer, they often get an instant download if they walk away from the screen to bake cookies, go for a walk, or make tea. The key is stepping out of what they were doing, surrendering, and tapping into flow to allow the answers to bubble up.

The more we practice writing without ego and surrendering to flow, the easier it is to get into that place and create with a sense of letting go and allowing what needs to come through.

The more you find yourself in that flow state, the more easily you'll get into it. But how do you find the time and space for feel-good flow when you've got your work, writing projects, family, life, and sleep?

Sometimes it's squeezing flow into the cracks of your day — a slow lunch or a five-minute journaling session with your tea or before bed. When we think we don't have time for flow is when we need it most. That's why scheduling flow is the best way to make it happen — just like writing.

Since flow isn't a "nice to have" but rather an essential — both for our well-being and for our craft — how about making it a priority?

To find more flow, get in the habit of scheduling time for flow first — before you do anything else.

Even if you find that state in various ways, putting fifteen minutes on your calendar every day as a chance to practice flow will help set the stage for the rest of your day.

JOURNAL PROMPTS

1. What are you hesitant about writing, creating, or sharing?
2. Look at your list of writing projects — are you writing them because you want to or feel you have to?
3. When was the last time you noticed yourself lose track of time? What were you doing?
4. What are five things you love doing that you could do for hours? Can you schedule one of those things this week?
5. What have you written in a state of flow? Revisit that writing and see if you can tap into the flow you found there.

CHAPTER 19
HOW TO TACKLE DIFFERENT TYPES OF WRITING

Each of the topics in this chapter could be a book on its own. My intention is to give you just enough detail to get going. If you haven't already learned from what you've read so far, this book is about starting and taking small actions without knowing entirely how the finished product will look.

There are many ways to write, publish, and share your writing. What you'll find here is some of my favorite advice I share with clients and in my writing community.

WEBSITE COPY

If you've been working on your website for longer than you care to admit, this advice will help you finally stop fussing with it.

I've shared the advice you're about to read in this chapter with hundreds of business owners — and I hear back from many of them that this advice helped them make those final tweaks to their websites so they could get it out there, and confidently start handing out business cards and sharing the link.

Many of these people have never paid me a dollar and

aren't in my writing community. I tell you this to remind you that you can get started with your website copywriting today.

I also want to remind you that if you run a service-based business and most of your clients come to you from referrals, your website will not be the first thing that gets them to take action. The thing that spurred these potential clients into action was their business bestie raving about your awesomeness.

Your website often serves as a business card — to show off your expertise, stand out, and build credibility. The website designers I've worked with all recommend first getting your copy in place. So before you focus on logos, color palettes, fonts, and branding, write your copy first. Yes, you might make some tweaks as you finalize your visuals — that's all part of the intuitive process.

It's helpful for a web designer to create around your words. And if you have to choose one investment of your time, energy, or money — invest in your copy first and design later. If you're just getting started in business, you likely need more data or experience to inform a designer or copywriter — I always tell people to write their copy first, work with people, get experience, and then start taking action toward hiring someone to help.

This section will help you write (or rewrite) your website from start to finish — whether you're just getting started or you're on your tenth rewrite.

Yes, you *can* write your website! Let's do this!

First lesson: Your website isn't about you. Well, it *is* technically about you. But your potential client only cares about how you can help them. People want to know what's in it for them. We all just like reading about ourselves. Your prospects are landing on your website to see the problem you solve and if you're a good fit for them, not to learn about your life story or favorite breakfast, or to get to know your fur babies.

The trick is to clearly communicate what you do in the words they would use. You're going to talk about what you can do for your reader by speaking directly to them.

Before we dive into what needs to go on each of your website's main pages, you first need to speak your people's language.

How to start speaking your client's language:

1. Pull up a blank document and call it "client words."
2. Write down every phrase ideal clients say to you. These are the exact words they use when complaining about their problems to their friends, what they say they really want, and what keeps them staring at the ceiling at 2:00 a.m. These are the things they say to you on discovery calls, intake forms, and in online groups when they're looking for solutions to their problems. This is what they say *before* they've hired you and know your brilliance.
3. Review and update these words every time you have a client interaction — this will be a living, breathing document that will evolve over time. And every time you work with someone new, you'll get new information to inform your copy.
4. Use these words and expressions every time you write anything for your website, blog, or social media.

Finally, before you start writing, let's talk about all of the advice floating around about niching your audience. (And, for the record, it's pronounced "neesh" not "nitch" — it's not something that needs scratching.) Some marketing gurus tell you that you need to have a super-specific niche, or you won't appeal to anyone. They often say, "If you try to market to everyone, you'll sell to no one." I call BS. When I first started my business, I wrote for anyone who'd hire me: C-suite executives, start-up tech companies, real estate agents, software companies, astrologers, naturopathic doctors. I still write for a pretty broad audience — and I enjoy every second of it. The one thing they all have in common is that they're creative, and they either don't have time to write or they need support. You can serve a broad audience right out of the gate, and until the market changes or you change your mind — carry on. When you commit to a niche, know that you can change your niche as you have insights and develop further.

Let's start with your Intuitive Intro.

Before you write anything public-facing, start with a short and sweet, Intuitive Intro.

The Intuitive Intro is your clear and confident answer to the question "What do you do?" It's your elevator pitch, your one-liner, your super short bio.

Whatever you call it, it's what you *do.* It's the impact you have on people.

Specifically, in the business world, it's what you and your business do to earn an income and who you do it for. And I've seen it trip up even the most confident CEOs.

Your Intuitive Intro is a natural-sounding, authentic-feeling statement about what you do and who you serve. That's it.

Your Intuitive Intro is not:

- All the copy on your website crammed into a run-on sentence

- A pitch to get you a job, sale, or client
- Your professional bio
- Written in stone forever and ever

Most importantly: Your Intuitive Intro doesn't define you or put you in a box. It's simply an ever-evolving message.

Important: your Intuitive Intro is about what you offer. The person reading or hearing your intro — whether they're a potential client, partner, contractor, or podcast host — cares about understanding what you do and how you can help them. Whether it's to work with you or pass your name along to someone who needs you, your skills, or your product.

People want to know how what you do relates to them. We all like reading about ourselves, so the more you can make your "what you do" statement focus on your reader, the better it will land.

The trick with your Intuitive Intro is to clearly communicate what you do in your client's exact words, making it easy for them to talk about you (in a good way, of course!).

Why write using your potential client's words?

It's an act of service to make your message easy to understand. If you use your words and not your client's, there could be a disconnect. It's like speaking a foreign language to them. You know so much more about how you help your clients. Your clients don't need to know all that. Using the exact words your clients use helps them to feel seen, heard, and understood. It shows them that they can trust you — you speak the same language after all.

Your Intuitive Intro will be the guiding light of your sales copy, so write the intro that corresponds to what you're going to sell.

If you have more than one ideal client audience or work in

various ways, choose *one* for this exercise and then come back and repeat the instructions for your next offer.

Your Intuitive Intro has three elements. You may not need all three. But you'll write all three then put them together.

1. Who you are — this is your title, if appropriate, or whatever you call yourself
2. The struggle bus you help your clients get off or what they want
3. What shiny results you deliver

Let's break them down one at a time. Step one: Who in the world *are* you? *I'm a [title/what you do]*.

This is all about what you call yourself. And this is the time to keep it super simple and avoid getting fancypants. This means if you're a life coach and your potential clients would search the web for "life coach," then, for the love of salty chocolate, call yourself a life coach.

If you're a consultant, writer, editor, developer, beekeeper, stylist, designer, bookkeeper, health coach, call yourself this. Dreaming up a fancy title for yourself in an attempt to stand out in a sea of samesies will only leave peeps scratching their heads.

When you're speaking your Intuitive Intro, this will be your opening statement. You'll drop this line, and if listeners want to know more, they'll ask questions.

As an example, because I'm a copywriter, coach, and author, I won't spit all this out in one go. Usually, I state, "I'm a writer." And if they give more than a flying fudgesicle, they'd ask, "Oh, what kind?" or "Do you write books?" And then I get specific.

This is your reminder that your Intuitive Intro is a conversation starter. It's never a time for you to rattle off where you graduated from college or how many awards you've won. That belongs on your resume or long bio.

Remember that you may not even have a super clear title for what you do. This is when you skip your title completely (because labels certainly don't matter here) and jump into step two, who you help. And who you serve is way more important than what you call yourself.

Example: I help business owners write website copy.

Step two: Who do *you* serve? *I [work with/serve/help] [people/business owners/entrepreneurs/CEOs/visionaries/cats/unicorns] who [struggle with/are frustrated by/are totally over/are tired of] [problem #1], [optional problem #2], [optional problem #3].*

This part is all about the struggle bus your prospect is on, what they're craving, or the main issue you help them solve.

Here, again, you'll use the *actual words* your people use to describe how they're feeling. And again (I say this a lot, so maybe you've heard this before), this is the unfancy way to talk about how they're feeling. These are the literal words they say to their business besties when they complain about their problems.

Sure, you might help your clients with a dozen problems — choose your top one to three and focus on those.

Now, step three: what do you help them do? *I [help them/support them with/create/make things] [describe what they say they want] so that they can tap into [what they really, really want].*

Now, you're a pro at what you do. You've got the street cred and the big brain. And when your prospects come to you with a problem, you know that what they *say* their problem is actually runs much, much deeper. But they don't know this yet, so if you tell them what you know they need but they aren't aware of it yet, there will be a disconnect.

For example, you're a coach who helps business owners organize their business, but what you really do is help them fall in love with their businesses again. Now, if your Intuitive Intro talked about how you teach entrepreneurs how to love their business, you'd likely end up with crickets. Because what they're looking for now is organization, so they can feel productive and get shit done.

Even if it feels plain, boring, or beige, you're connecting with what your potential client says they want. And in their words. Are you noticing the theme yet?

When you think you've landed on an Intuitive Intro you love (or even just like quite a bit — remember, we're not perfectionists here) let it sit for a few days to make sure. I see many entrepreneurs trying to force their way there, trying to get it "right." There is no right — the goal is to get to good enough. Good enough means 80 percent. You'll tweak it as you get real-life experience.

My Intuitive Intro has changed dozens of times since I started my business, and I use different versions for different purposes.

Here's mine at this moment, keeping you in mind:

"I'm an author, copywriter, writing coach and the founder of The Intuitive Writing School. I help creatives move past writer's block and perfectionism so they can finish their important work. I also support business owners in finding their authentic voice so they can make an impact on the world.

Whether it's for your website, a program launch, or your book, I'll help you get the words out."

Let's start writing the rest of your website.

That Intuitive Intro stuff is no joke! You might be tired — your brain needs a rest after doing this. Keep in mind, rest isn't something you need to earn — you innately need to rest to keep your brain focused. You can get started on the rest of your website copy before you've finalized your intro — get to 80 percent good enough and keep moving forward. You'll have insights every time you take action. So keep taking action. Feel free to move ahead and come back to your intro.

I firmly believe: The order in which you write your website pages matters.

Almost every business owner I talk to makes this mistake — I did too. You start with the first page that your website visitors see — your home page.

Your home page is your foyer, your entryway — telling people they're in the right place and what to do next. Until you've at least written sales copy (which is 99.9 percent focused on your potential clients' words), you don't yet have the language to write the home page.

Write the home page last. When you do, you'll have so many golden nuggets from your other pages that writing your home page will be a breeze.

Write your sales page first.

If you have only *one* page on your website, let it be the one that can highlight what you do and make you money. You can ship this one first and launch the rest as they're ready.

While your home and about pages are important, your sales page is the first step before bringing dollars into your bank account. This means you'll spend the most time writing and editing your offer copy.

So, how do you describe this thing you do? *Uh, I'm really smart, and I've created this amazing thing, so um . . . buy it, okay?*

Those might not be the actual words you'd use, but maybe

it sounds that way in your head. Selling your services or products can feel completely authentic — it doesn't need to feel salesy or slimy.

Think about your offer as serving your audience. Selling is awesome — it means you're helping. Once you understand what goes into a sales page and tap into your customer's language, writing it gets so much easier. And dare I say, fun? Most importantly, it sells!

Before you start writing, I'm going to walk you through writing prompts for the four components your sales page needs: First, your customer's pain or problem; second, their opportunity or transformation; third, why you're the one to help them; and, finally, what they'll get from your service or product.

Intuitive Writing Tip

Before you begin writing sales copy, take pen to paper and outline who it's for and why it's great. I always recommend pen to paper for turning off your logical mind and letting your body guide the way.

1. Pain, problem, or connection

What's your customer's big problem? Or thing they're missing? It may not be a "pain" or "problem" but something they want that they don't have yet. Here you'll describe how your prospects feel using the exact words they use to describe their problem at the point when they're ready to look for help. Remember that file of client language you created already? Refer back to that.

- How is your prospect feeling right now?

- What do they search online when looking for solutions to their problem?
- What do they tell their friends they want?
- How does the problem make them feel?
- Are other parts of their lives affected now?
- How do they feel when they're in the middle of their problem?

2. Pleasure, opportunity, or transformation

Now that you've described your prospect's pain in all its glory, pretend they no longer have the problem. Poof! The problem is gone! (and psst – you're the one who's gonna help take it away.) What do they secretly crave? What is it that they say they want?

- What does their life look like without their problem?
- How do they feel without this issue?
- What can they look forward to now?
- What feels amazing with this problem totally gone?
- What other areas of their lives are better now?
- Looking back on the pain they felt earlier, how does each part feel now?

3. Why you're the one to help them

Who are you, and who do you support? Why is working with you the bomb.com? Keep this to just a few sentences and relevant to your prospect at the moment when they're spinning in the cyclone of their problem. Hint: this will come from your Intuitive Intro.

You might also add:

- Why should they listen to you? Have you been there before?
- How can you show them that you understand their situation?
- Who do you work with? These are your favorite people that you can also deliver amazing results to.

4. What they get

Now that you've described their personal brand of pain, what pleasure could look and feel like, and why you're the one to trust, tell them the tangible things they get from working with you. Leave out your twelve-step process here unless they're specifically shopping for a twelve-step process.

- WIIFM? What's in it for me? What will your customers get in the way of benefits?
- What tactical components do your clients get (three one-on-one calls, unlimited emails, etc.)?
- How will their lives improve?
- What can they do now?
- In their words, what do they say they want? Show them how they get it.

With your brainstorm ready, you can arrange the best of each area into a sales page. You'll also add essential offer components like a great name, the investment (generally list it on the page if it's less than $20,000), and what steps they'll take when they're ready to work with you.

A note on introducing your price: I always say "investment" to create a positive internal idea. When we say "cost" or "price," it can make people feel like they're losing something.

An investment is something that pays you back someday. And, it's an investment worth making!

Just like on all the other pages of your website, tell them the steps they need to take next to work with you or buy your product. You might think it's obvious (and it probably is). Pretend they need hand-holding. Making their life easier will make them grateful to you. Make it easy for customers to pay you.

This is also a great place to feature testimonials of people who have bought your thing. Feature those quotes right here on the page.

Write your about page next.

This is all about you — but only as it relates to your reader.

Your about page is probably the second most popular page on your website, followed by your home page (track your website analytics regularly). Once your reader decides they're in the right place, they want to know who you are.

The goal of your about page: Build trust and deepen connections by telling your story.

People buy from people they know, like, and trust (especially that last one), so please don't half-ass your about page. Put your full ass into it. And not literally, unless you have *that* kind of website.

Before diving into your story, write about your reader. Do this by crafting a few "you" statements based on how your reader is feeling right now.

If you wrote your sales page first (like I recommend), you'll have some of this language handy.

Here are some examples:

- "You're sick of writing, and you just wish someone would do it for you."

- "If only someone would tell you what to write."
- "Writing about yourself is so freaking hard!"

When you read a business owner's about page, sometimes you're impressed – maybe they made you giggle, spit out your coffee, or even offended you slightly.

This is great! Their writing caused a reaction. And when it comes to your writing, your goal is to get a reaction out of your readers – you just need to figure out what kind you want.

Use these writing prompts to help shape your about page into a work of art you'll be excited to share.

Take pen to paper and use these questions to help you brainstorm:

- What did you believe to be true about your industry before you started working in it?
- What do you believe today?
- Why do you do this work?
- What lights you up?
- How are you different from others in your industry?
- How do you feel when you sit down to work each day?
- Did you have a low point or aha moment that brought you to where you are today? Did you experience a bunch of them?
- What experiences do you have that make you incredible at your job?
- What do clients constantly compliment you on?
- What are people always asking you for advice on?
- What's your theme song for your life right now?
- What would people be surprised to know about you?

With your brainstorm ready, look at the highlights and consider what pieces of your story apply to your audience and how that relates to helping clients in your business.

Give your brainstorm at least a day to rest between visiting these prompts and writing for your website.

Take your prospects on a journey through your aha moments. You might have one big one or a series of events that led you to where you are today. As you get going, don't worry yet about which pieces you want to tell. We want to keep moving here. Note the stories you think you'll include and flesh them out later. When you start editing your about page, you might decide that some stories no longer fit, or some are simply making it too long.

Intuitive Writing Tip

Save any stories you remove from your about page! You can use them for future blog posts, email, or social media content.

Tell only the stories that are relevant to how you came to do what you do today and why it matters.

Sometimes clients ask me why their readers need to know details about their lives. Well, first, they don't need all the details. Only write about the particulars you're comfortable sharing. Sharing pieces of your journey with your readers helps them spark a connection with you and is an important step in learning to trust you as an authority in your industry.

Your readers are reading your about page and your stories as a way to look for a natural connection with you — *Oh, she likes matcha just as much as I do! Whoa, we grew up in the same state! Or whoa, she also loves going barefoot!* It's those little connection points that your readers remember.

They're also looking at your story as a metaphor for their potential transformation. They're not reading your story to judge you (and if they are, that's on them). They're reading to see that it's possible for them to get where they want to go based on your journey. It doesn't need to look exactly the same as theirs — they only need to see that there was a transformation.

Your about page is a way for you to stand out in a sea of third-person, acronym, and jargon-filled bios and a fun way to share your values.

End your about page story with a call to action.

What should your reader do now that they just read your story? Tell them precisely what to do. You could ask them to sign up for your newsletter, read your top blog posts, buy your stuff, or grab a spot on your calendar.

Include a professional bio if you'll be speaking or featured on other blogs or podcasts. This will be a few short paragraphs, written in the third person, that someone can easily cut and paste from your website. Use your Intuitive Intro written in the third person to get started. The next time someone asks you, "Can you send me your bio?" — you'll be ready.

Depending on your industry, you may need to flash some credentials. List your certifications if your clients care about these. Usually, you can compile them in a bulleted list near the end of your about page.

Finally, write your home page.

Now that you've done all the hard brainwork of writing your sales and about pages, you have a huge well of words to draw upon to inspire your home page.

Your home page has one job — let readers know they're in the right place.

Unless readers land on your website from a blog post or one of your offers, they're going to see your home page first.

Your home page is the curb appeal for the rest of your website. If the door handle is hanging off, your grass is overgrown with weeds, and you have a Halloween welcome mat in July, visitors will quickly turn around, thinking, "This must be the wrong place."

Tell them they're in the right place and encourage them to get comfortable and stay awhile.

Your home page should include:

- Your opt-in for your email newsletter (if you have one) with a compelling invitation to sign up that's not, "Hi, join my list!" No one wants to be on a list. They care about what they get. If possible, include this above the fold — before you start scrolling and at the bottom — because if they made it to the bottom of the page, maybe they want to hang out with you in their inbox.
- Tell them what they'll get, how often, and how their life will be better for handing over their email address.
- What you do, who you help, how you help them, and the results they'll get from working with you. This is your Intuitive Intro again. That writing exercise is coming in handy!
- Tell them what to do! Instead of leaving them awkwardly hanging out in your foyer, tell them to read your blog, grab a freebie, send you an email, learn about how to work with you, book a call, or whatever else you want them to do.

Intuitive Writing Tip
This advice applies to everything you write – ever. STOP working on your website copy if you start to feel shitty. Revisit Chapters 6 and 8, and then return to the page. When you feel good, your reader feels good.

BLOGS

"*Should I start a blog?*" I get this question a lot – especially from new business owners. Almost always, my question back to them is this: "Do you *want* to blog?"

People are usually surprised when I put the ball back in their court. It's as if no one has ever asked them before. When did we decide that it was okay to put our wants last and instead follow some fearless leader's advice and do what they say?

If you want to blog, blog.

If you love to talk, start a podcast.

And . . . you can do both. But I recommend starting with one, so you don't get overwhelmed and stop creating altogether. This way, you can stay focused on one before moving onto the next.

Intuitive Writing Tip
If you're thinking of writing a book someday and aren't clear on the topic, start a blog today. That blog can inspire a good chunk of your book.

It's true that a blog can help you position yourself as the go-to expert in your industry and build trust with your readers. It's also good for SEO (Search Engine Optimization) – so web search engines can find you easily. When you're regularly adding new content in the form of articles to your website, it tells search engines that you've got new stuff — that they should pay attention to this site because it's getting regular updates.

Here are some questions to help you decide if a blog is for you:

- Do you like writing?
- Do you want to blog?
- Do you have ideas to share?
- Are you receiving the same questions from your clients all the time?
- Are you an internal processor and get to your answers by writing?
- Does blogging support your business goals?
- Do you want to write a book one day? You could use your blog content to help shape your book (many of the chapters in *Unfussy Life and* this book started as blog posts).
- Will your blog help potential clients get to know you and your work better?

The choice is yours. When you create with intention and put your words into the world in the way only you can, it will feel easier and have a greater chance of sparking authentic connection.

Here are some simple ways to get started (or restarted) on a blog project:

Decide how you prefer to create.

Do you love the feel of writing with a pen and paper? Start writing your blog posts longhand, then type them out. This is a great way to do your first edit.

Do the words fall out of your fingers, or do you prefer to talk stuff out? Sometimes I'm so tired of staring at a screen I'll take a walk to talk an idea out on my phone. This can be a strategy you play with occasionally or all the time if you really love it. Then when it comes time to review and edit, you'll have some grammar and copy editing to do, but it will be much easier than starting from a blank page.

Notice what feels best to you because the best way for it to come out of you is the best way to make it happen.

Brainstorm what to write about.

Look at what you're selling, and then back into your offers – what does a reader need to know or believe *before* they'll book a consult with you or buy from you?

Your blog posts can be:

- Stories
- Reviews
- Lists
- Steps or instructions on how to accomplish something
- Bullets of ideas to explore
- A combination of these, depending on what you're writing about

Choose your blogging frequency.

Consider your launch schedule or new services you're rolling out. Do you have a program you launch four times a year? Back into that launch with your blog content. Maybe you blog weekly and want to incorporate articles that will support your launching efforts. Include up to six blog posts that help sell your offer. If you don't launch and provide services all year long, what do people need to know, feel, or believe before they'll sign up with you? Your answers to these questions are your content.

Choose a schedule for posting and stick to it. Even if it's once a month (that's great!), get started there. Once you're comfortable with monthly posting, ramp up to every other week. From there, blog weekly if you like, or even a few times a week.

Now it's time to write. Let's look at the components of your blog post, especially how you open, how you hold attention through the middle, and how you close your posts.

How to open a blog post.

When you start a blog post, how often do you write the first few words, then the first sentence, then decide you don't like it? I get it — I do this a lot. You might decide to come back to your opening lines later. When writing blog posts, there's no need to write them in the order people read.

The first few words of your blog post are part of your first impression. After the title (which we'll talk about in a moment), it's what makes your reader want to keep reading. Your opening line can make or break your blog post.

Here are some ideas for a strong first impression:

- Ask a question to pique your reader's curiosity. It could be a question they were too afraid or embarrassed to ask.
- Start with a fact. Just make sure your stat is both relevant and correct. Link to your reliable source. If the statistic is interesting, unique, or maybe even shocking, you'll provoke your reader to pay

attention. It's also a way to offer data that an analytical reader will find appealing.

- Use a famous quote. At least when you use a quote, you don't need to come up with the right words – they already exist. Digging for excerpts can be time-consuming, so keep a running list of quotes that catch your eye. Make sure you attribute the passage to the right person.
- Paint a picture with words and give your readers a mental image to get their imaginations fired up. You can do this by starting with statements like "Imagine you're . . ." "Picture this . . ." or "Do you remember?"
- Forget words altogether and start with a picture. A picture is worth a thousand words, or at the very least, can replace the first thirty words of a blog. I prefer to use my own images in my blog posts and around my website. Stock photos are just so – stocky. If you have an artistic side, create your own illustrations.
- Get to the point. Readers don't have time to sift through your 1,800-word blog post to figure out the point. Do your readers a favor and tell them right away. "Coffee enemas are life" or "Smoking weed is making you dumb."
- Tease a story. Storytelling is a skill that takes practice. The good news is that because you're human, you have the innate ability to tell stories – it's how we learn and connect. Some examples:

It was the first time I chose the wine on the top shelf.
I slept right through the most important alarm of my life.
I closed my eyes and dropped my head.

A fedora, purple suit, and cauliflower rice.
I sat there in a puddle of tears.

How to write the middle of a blog post.

This is the meat (or, ahem, tofu) of your story. This is where you'll share information. But how long should a post be? If you've ever fallen down a web search rabbit hole trying to find out, you probably already know by now that there's no straightforward answer.

Your post should be as long as you need it to be to get your point across — no shorter, no longer. If your blog post is nearing eight thousand words, break it into a series or consider writing a mini-book.

Blog posts range from three hundred to three thousand words. SEO typically favors those around two thousand words — because, as you can guess, readers are on those pages longer. The longer a reader is on a page, the longer the search engine's algorithm is noticing that they're hanging out there — giving the impression that what people will find on your website is good shit.

How to wrap up your blog post.

You get to the end of a blog post that you thoroughly enjoyed reading. It was well thought out, maybe inspired you to try something new, or it just made you chortle so hard that your iced latte shot out your nose.

When you get to the end of your blog or article, tell your reader what to do next. Here are some ideas:

- Wrap up your blog post with a teaser for your next article.

- Ask a question and invite them into a conversation if you have comments on your blog. A note on comments: I removed the comments function from my blog because I prefer to spend my time creating and living instead of blocking bots and moderating spammers. You can always invite them to hop over to your social media page to comment or invite them to reply to you privately via email.
- Part with a memorable quote.
- Write a specific call to action (CTA). What precisely do you want your reader to do next? You can tell them, "Hey, if you liked this, you'll probably like [this blog post], or [this blog post]." I like to suggest other articles in groups of either three or five.
- Tell readers where to get more. Ask them to sign up for your newsletter.
- Include a unique discount code or offer a secret bonus to your blog readers.
- Promote your products or services. A single blog post might just be the nudge your reader needs to buy from you. Even though your blog isn't technically a sales page, something you touch on in an article may speak directly to their heart, and they realize how much they need what you have.

Here are some sample questions and prompts you can use to include at the bottom of your blog post:

- Are you struggling with [the problem you outlined]? You might like this [add a link to your product/service].

- Have you tried all of these things, and stuff still sucks bojangles? This might be for you [link to your offer/product].
- Are you ready for [amazing, kickass thing you offer]? Get your hands on this! [link to your thing].
- Would this feel like a dream to you? [Product/service name] could take you from [crappy state] to [amazeballs state].

Intuitive writers are mindful of (not obsessed with) SEO.

I didn't even look at SEO until several years into my business and a handful of years after earning a full-time income. I hired an SEO consultant to audit my website and make recommendations because mine needed a fresh start. The SEO industry is like the Wild West — if you do look for the help of a consultant, look to people you trust for recommendations.

SEO didn't matter for my business for years. As a service-based business that only requires a small number of clients to fill my client roster, 99.95 percent of my clients come to me through referrals. Don't underestimate the power of doing good work, asking for referrals, and then repeating it over and over. It wasn't until I was seven years into running my business that someone booked a consult call because they found my website via Google.

Writing for SEO might feel boring AF — especially if you're a creative or empathic with a strong intuition. I need to write about things that feel exciting. I need to follow that excitement, answer questions, and not just write about something because I "should" do it for the keywords — barf.

When you're first getting started, think about the words people will naturally search to find you. Over time, track these words and see how people land on your website. When you notice trends and certain keywords, double down on them and use them more.

I invested in my SEO strategy more than a year after starting my writing community. Now that I sell templates, self-paced courses, and am growing a community, this calls for an increased volume of eyeballs on my website. That can come from organic growth and website traffic to attract new members (but still — it's growing mainly from member referrals today). If you have a digital products business or require a larger volume of people and your business isn't referral-based, SEO can be smart to explore. But don't let your SEO research stop you from starting to blog.

How to write powerful headlines.

You just spent 2.7 hours writing your latest blog post. Now it's time to come up with a catchy title.

You decide you'll just call it whatever so you can be done with it. You've already been thinking about it for thirty minutes, and you've got other shit to do.

Hold up! Give your headline the love it deserves. If you give your blog post a piddly headline, you could be doing it a disservice.

A killer headline tempts readers to click and read the rest.

Not putting time into your headline is like pouring your Grey Poupon inside a generic yellow mustard bottle. Bleh. No one is going to know what spicy goodness is sitting inside!

Stay open to great headlines. They might come to you:

1. Before you begin. Suppose you think of a fantastic headline before you even start writing — awesome!

This will help guide your writing. If not, don't stress — you've got time.

2. In the middle of writing your article. Out of nowhere, a great headline smacks you in the face. As you get ideas, list them as they come to you; you'll refine them later. I love when this happens because it's my favorite effortless way to name things.
3. Once you're finished writing. As you do a final read-through, start creating some options. This is because once you dive in and begin exploring a topic, you might take a U-turn and write in an entirely different direction.

Days, weeks, or years later. Hey — as you improve as a writer and get better at your headline writing skills, you'll look back at old ones and see opportunities to write stronger ones. Go ahead and change the headline later. I recommend leaving the URL alone unless you have a tight process for updating everywhere you might have linked to that blog.

Here are some headline-crafting tips:

1. Be open to a big brainstorm. Write as many that come to mind. If they start going in another direction, save them for something else.
2. WIIFM? That is, "what's in it for me?" How will your reader's life be better after reading your article? Tell them in the headline so they can glance at it and decide for themselves.
3. Keep it simple. Never sacrifice clarity to attempt to be clever. A confused reader skims right past. As

long as you're addressing a specific benefit, you have permission to keep it simple and readable.

4. Find your image first. If a picture is worth a thousand words, you can use it to inspire your title.
5. Add some power to grab your reader. Once you have some headline ideas, play with different emotional or sensory words. Power words add a dose of persuasion and engage your reader because they spark feelings and help them see, hear, sense, and even smell your copy. To come up with power words, think about how you want your reader to feel when they read your writing. Do you want them to feel excited, inspired, or empowered? Once you have these feelings, you can explore some words that pop.
6. Create a swipe file of titles and headlines that grab your attention. Stand in line at the supermarket and see which magazine headlines stand out. When you're scrolling social media, make a habit of noting any headlines that tugged on your eyeballs or heartstrings. The more you start paying attention to great headlines, the more easily you'll be able to pull the fantastic ones out of thin air.

Here's some headline-making inspiration for you with my favorite snack as the star:

- 11 Raw Cacao and Artisanal Tea Pairings
- 11 Signs You're Not Eating Enough Chocolate
- 11 Surprising Ways to Dazzle Your Guests with Chocolate
- 11 Unexpected Chocolate and Fruit Pairings

- 11 Completely Acceptable Reasons to Drink Cacao Every Day
- 11 Easy Ways to Ruin an Expensive Bag of Ceremonial Raw Cacao
- 11 Easy Ways to Make Raw Cacao Deliciously Sippable
- 11 Ways to Delight Your Dinner Guests with a Chocolate Tasting
- The Smart Way to Build Your Chocolate Collection
- 11 Important Lessons after 11 Bars of Dark Chocolate
- 11 Sure-Fire Ways to Pick a Winning Bar of Chocolate
- 11 Little-Known Facts about Chocolate
- 11 Mistakes That Make You Look Like a Chocolate Amateur
- 11 Inspiring Quotes about Enjoying Chocolate
- 11 Ways to Seduce Your Guests with Chocolate-Infused Desserts
- 11 Ways to Impress Your Guests with Your Chocolate Know-How
- 11 Ways to Get Your Followers to Fall Head-Over-Heels in Love with Chocolate
- 11 Happy Endings: How to End a Meal with the Perfect Chocolate
- 11 Reasons to Stop Saving the Good Chocolate for a Special Occasion
- How to Eat Vegetables When You'd Rather be Eating Chocolate
- Think This Souffle Is Chocolate? It Has a Surprise Ingredient!
- Chocolate as Healer

The secret to writing great headlines is that there is no secret. You only need to play. The more you practice coming up with compelling headlines, the better you'll get.

SOCIAL POSTS

If you want to use social media, fantastic, here are some tips. And if you choose not to use social media, that's great too. You don't have to. I've been using social media consistently for a long time, and I never scratch my head wondering what to post.

That's because I use a simple trick: I share the content of whatever I publish on my blog all week or month long.

Mine that blog or podcast you put so much effort into and repurpose for days! Even if you publish one or two blog posts a month, pull out key snippets, pieces, audience prompts, common questions, and quotes and share them later. This has saved me hours of staring at my screen pondering what to write.

Here's how it might look for a weekly piece of long-form content. Think of the one piece of content you create each week as your anchor.

And then . . .

On publishing day — share the link to the article or podcast to your newsletter and each social media channel that you're active on.

Then, daily for the next week, or spread over two or more weeks, share a snippet, a lesson, a quote, or a question based on that original anchor content.

Return to your old content during key months, pull out pivotal pieces, rewrite the captions, change up the images, and post away. No one's going to remember that you wrote about a similar topic sixteen months ago.

While you might feel like you're constantly talking about

the same thing, this is okay — it's essential to getting your message out.

And you'll be sharing the same core message with slightly different words and the core theme all week long.

Intuitive Writing Tip

Relentless creation can get tiring, especially if you're forcing it. Embrace the cyclical process and go back and reuse your writing exponentially. Make all those words work even harder for you by reusing and repurposing.

Each month, I recommend checking your website traffic analytics. If your social content rarely converts to website visits, revisit your strategy before you consider pulling the plug.

Other ways to keep a consistent social media presence:

- Review questions from your prospects, clients, and customers — what do they ask about? Summarize each question into a post.
- Comb your entire website — pull out key quotes, snippets about you, your process, your story, and create social posts from there. Just be sure to go in and engage at least a few times a week.
- Batching your social posts once a month or so, like batching your food prep, makes it easy. In addition to creating social posts based on my latest blog posts, I review questions people ask, themes I see in books and online, then I create a bank of text-based images. Then, each day when I go to post, I look at my bank and intuitively decide what to share.

- Use social media schedulers. This way, you can batch all your posts in roughly an hour a month and to your social media followers, you're there, staying top-of-mind.

EMAILS

Every once in a while, the social media platforms have outages. And every time this happens you see people panic – *but I was going to launch my course today!*

Looking to social media as the be-all-end-all for getting your words out is a dangerous idea. I recommend keeping your eggs in multiple baskets, and growing and using your email list.

Now, you might worry that your list is "too small" – that depends. If you have a service-based business or offer a premium service, you don't need thousands of subscribers. As a done-for-you copywriter, most of my copywriting clients don't opt-in to my email newsletter first. They came to me through referrals and skipped joining my list because they didn't want weekly writing advice; they wanted someone to write for them.

And if you have thirty people on your list, imagine those people in your living room. They came to hear what you have to say. I'm guessing your couch seats five people max – and that's if they're sitting cheek-to-cheek, and the rest of your living room is standing room only. Now start speaking and feed the thirty people who are there.

Regular email newsletters to your audience are a way to build trust, share a message, and help people get to know you. Whatever you decide to send, just send it consistently – whether that's monthly, weekly, or daily.

I like to write my emails within a day or so of sending them out. I rarely schedule newsletters way in advance. There's so much more power in my message when I sit down to write in the moment. When I write something weeks ahead of time, I'm creating with the energy of that week, which will be very different from future weeks.

Here are some strategies to work into your emails – whether they're email newsletters or sales emails:

- Share your latest blog post or podcast. Cut and paste your entire blog post into your email. This strategy is helpful if you know your readers will mainly read in their inboxes. How much do you like clicking on a link that takes you out of your inbox – especially if you're reading on your phone? Avoid this strategy if you want to train your readers to get used to clicking something.
- Personalize it. Add your subscriber's name, and not just in your greeting – look for opportunities to weave it into the email. Occasionally, experiment with using your reader's name in the subject line. You'll also speak directly to your reader and say things like, "Last week I told you about . . ." and not, "Hey everyone!" Because even though it feels like you're emailing a group of people, they don't sit around and read your email together. Write to one reader, the reader who's most excited to learn from you.
- Write a brief introduction teasing out what they'll learn when they read the rest. Make it compelling enough to click. Keeping these intros super brief (under three hundred words or so) is a great way to entice people to read further.
- In most cases, make sure there's only one thing you want readers to click. When people have too many options, they may click on something that you

didn't really want them to click on. You could have saved that for another email.

- Sign off with an invitation. Invite your reader to share your article by clicking on the link to your blog post. Invite them to connect, reply, do a secret dance, or share it on social media with a hashtag.
- Give them more. If your reader enjoys what they read, give them more reasons to keep reading. Suggest some other posts, interviews, books, or places they can get their fill of the wisdom you share.
- Add personal touches and share things you love. Depending on what you sense your audience will love, your mood, or what's going on with nature's rhythm, you could add a link to the funniest video of pandas you've ever seen, a social post of a random act of kindness, a new service you're loving, the book on your nightstand, or even a haiku. I personally save all my best shares for email.
- Use round-up emails. If you're guest blogging on other platforms, have a series of podcast interviews in other places, and have events or workshops going on, a round-up is a simple way to share updates and provide value instead of emailing your list every time you have something to send, which could exhaust your readers. When you offer up a buffet of items for your readers to click on, you're giving them choices.
- Give thought to email subject lines. Just like the advice in the earlier section about naming things, you might decide on your subject line last. Test out which subject lines your audience likes to open most. And just like headlines out in the wild that

catch your attention, start a swipe file of email subject lines that you couldn't help but click and use them as inspiration for your emails.

To P.S. or not to P.S.? Short answer: Yes. The P.S. in your emails is ridiculously important. Here's why using one in your emails is a super-smart move:

- It trains your readers to look for exciting things
- It's great for skimmers — if you want your reader to do *one thing*, put it in the P.S.
- It makes your emails feel personal
- When used consistently, your reader *knows* that the best stuff is in the P.S.
- The fun things you share deepen your connection and trust with readers
- It's an effective way to reinforce a call to action
- It sums up what your email was about in one sentence
- It sells something
- It plants seeds for future offers, books, and events

What your P.S. is *not* for: Writing something super long or dropping a sales bomb when the rest of the email was to educate, entertain, or inspire. Put the call to action for sales in the email body.

What to include in your P.S.:

- Links to that social media picture of the best latte you ever had
- Links to a social post that spurred lots of great discussions
- A fun picture or quote you shared on Instagram

- Tease your next email, exciting offer, or event
- The current theme song for your life
- Videos of goats wearing pajamas
- An older piece of content that your reader would enjoy
- A reminder about what they just read
- The only action your reader needs to take after reading
- A playlist you love
- A new product or service you're currently obsessed with
- A nudge to invite a shift in their thinking
- A note addressing potential objections they might have
- The link you asked your reader to click in the email — a great idea to include it twice

P.S.: And if you're wondering what P.S. even means, it's postscript, abbreviated to P.S. The term comes from the Latin "post scriptum," an expression meaning "written after."

P.P.S.: You have full permission to write a P.P.S and P.P.P.S if you like.

BOOKS

Right before I published *Unfussy Life* in April 2021, I started to get the itch to write another book. Now, I was in the home stretch of publishing, and it would have been self-sabotage at its finest if I had jumped ship and focused on starting something new.

I wrote the very first, very shitty first draft of *Unfussy Life* in 2017 — it came out of me during my first NaNoWriMo. Read more about this writing challenge in Chapter 21. I knew I wanted to write this second book with more intuitive guidance and practical writing advice.

I love the idea of a creative container of thirty days and 50,000 words to get a bunch of focused writing work done. I still ran (even grew) my business and continued serving my clients while working on my book project.

I don't know if I'll ever be one of those writers who sits around and writes all day — and really, I don't think I want to. Sure, I love writing. I also love variety and task-switching throughout the day. Whether editing a client's SFD, coaching clients, writing a social post, or drafting a sales page for a new course — I love the creative inspiration that task-switching brings me.

The month that I drafted the very shitty preliminary draft of *Unfussy Life*, I didn't prep at all.

Meet 2017 book writing me:

Pick a random day in October, set a timer, play Metallica, and write thirty topic ideas on thirty index cards (my goal was to write a chapter a day).

Every day in November — write at least 1,667 words. I tracked my word count progress in a spreadsheet and created a new Google Doc for each chapter. No revisiting, no revising, no thinking — only super-fast writing.

I didn't plan ahead and continued publishing weekly blog and newsletter content — this aspect felt a little draining.

I skipped my morning pages habit, set my alarm for 5:00 a.m. most days, and got up to write before anyone else was awake.

I'd often go to a coffee shop to focus for an hour or so on weekends since the kids were home.

I let that book project sit for a year before I picked it up to edit it again. I edited it during NaNoWriMo 2018 — a whole year later. I did my editing first thing in the morning or when the kids were at their respective practices.

My process for writing *this* book:

This time, I prepared better, which set the stage for a stronger first draft.

Starting in August 2021 (three months before I'd begin writing), I started writing at least five hundred SFD words most weekdays for my blog. I revisited those drafts, polished and scheduled them for each week (or every other week) through October and November. Being ahead on my content writing helped me to focus on book writing. And if I needed to reorder any blog posts based on world events, astrological events, or just because I felt like it, I'd adjust them as needed.

Each week, I continued to send weekly newsletters to my email subscribers. It's usually based on whatever content I created for the blog that week. Sometimes the email would point to an older but relevant topic.

In addition to getting ahead on content-creation for my business, I dedicated August to dreaming and journaling about what this book would look like. I knew I wouldn't be mapping or putting anything into a Google Doc yet. During September, I planned and started outlining what it would look like. In October, I continued the prep.

Also, in October, I hired two book writing experts to help set me off on the right foot.

One was an editor and book coach who specializes in human design for writers. It was fascinating and gave me the reassurance I needed that I was already headed down the right path. The other person I hired was a book coach and editor to help me outline. We spent ninety minutes tuning into the energetics of this book — what it wanted to be — and deciding what flow made the most sense (even though we'd rearrange later).

My last few steps for prep in October:

- Blocking thirty minutes every day in November to write — sometimes that's all I'd do, and sometimes I'd start ahead of schedule or keep going afterward. I scheduled the session to happen with my writing community — every day — including on weekends. Some people thought I was nuts.
- I also blocked chunks of time and days I knew would be hectic — family traveling in for the US Thanksgiving, hockey tournaments, kids off school, and busy life.
- The days before starting to write, I made sure the house was stocked with healthy food and did some batch cooking to take my mind off meal prep.
- My former project manager days developed my love of a good project plan. This one lived in a spreadsheet — I added each section of the book as a line item, added a due date, created a separate Google Doc for each chapter, numbered it, and linked it in my sheet. Each day of writing, I knew exactly what section I'd be working on.

I continued to serve my writing community, private coaching clients, and copywriting clients. I welcomed about a dozen new community members, two retainer content-writing projects, a done-for-you copywriting project, and continued marketing with social posts and blog content I had prepared earlier that season.

We also had out-of-town guests and two hockey tournaments (yes, all in one month). On the second day of NaNoWriMo, we found out that our old American bulldog, Roland, had liposarcoma — cancer. I sensed that he had about two or three months left with us. It was a sad and heavy feeling, and I could easily see where I could have let that take my focus away.

November also saw me writing this book with Roland sleeping in his bed next to my chair, letting out the frequent fart, and getting extra cuddles from me every time I got up from my desk. *I have to share the synchronicity with you that as I revisited this exact paragraph in early 2022 for edits, Roland limped into my office to lay down behind my chair.*

This deliberate approach to book writing felt different from the pantsing I did a few years ago.

Pantsing worked fine for me then, and I'll always be winging it to some degree. It's how I love to create, and natural for the feminine — wild and creative, like the sea. Though it was frustrating many times during the editing process (my poor editor — but she says she loves this stuff), and the multiple times I revisited and reorganized it.

This time, the book's flow was clearer from the beginning. And I also know from experience that even if I go into the writing process with the best intentions, writing is an act of co-creating with the Divine, and the direction will likely shift while I'm writing. That's the magic of surrender.

I've already proved to my unconscious mind that I know how to write, edit, and publish a book. So doing it again, my brain is like, "Oh yeah, we know how to do this — we got this!" While it was often uncomfortable during the writing process the first time, I've created the container for the next book (and the next, and the next).

And that's the whole point. Until I started writing and publishing my blog weekly, I didn't have the container. Now, a decade later, blogging feels like breathing.

There are lots of ways to work on a book. For example, you can write blog posts throughout the year, then turn them into a book (with lots of editing). That's what comprised much of the foundation of this book. Over several years I'd been sharing writing advice — I had so much already at my fingertips that the initial creation was easier, though I also wrote many chapters from scratch.

As I jumped into writing this book on November 1 with my community — who were also kicking off writing projects — I asked members two questions:

1. How will you feel when you finish this project?
2. How will you celebrate?

I invite you to explore these questions before you begin writing your book.

I noted what people shared, and on December 1, I checked in. Did they feel that way? Why or why not? Did you remember to celebrate? So many people skip this step. Celebrating your focus and determination is a big deal and leads to more wins (more finished writing projects).

Before starting this book, I was having conversations with other entrepreneurs in my direct messages — they, too, had been feeling the pull to write a book.

Their questions all had a similar theme — how do you do it? How did you structure it? How do you start? How do you finish?

Some wanted to know the whole picture before they'd jump in.

The ones who were okay with uncertainty and diving into the unknown were the ones who joined us for most of the daily writing sessions, committed to their project over and over, and showed up to write it.

What these people weren't doing: Seeking validation or approval for their book project — which I don't give. That needs to come from inside.

It's so much easier to go into your book project with time on your calendar to write, an intuitive plan, and clarity on how you'll feel when finished.

At the same time, you don't want to over-plan. When you begin with a small window of clarity and trust that if you surrender to the process, you'll get the guidance you need. Importantly, you're leaving room for the magic to happen.

Kimberly joined my writing community to focus on business writing. And then a new belief unlocked something more.

> "I now believe that everyone can write. This was a big one for me. I joined the writing community to become more confident in writing blog posts and newsletters. I never dreamed I was good enough to write a book, but here I am. This never would have never happened without the mindset shift from being a part of this writing group.

In a little over a year, Kimberly not only wrote and published her first book but also contributed to a multi-author book. If you think you have a book in you "someday" — that day could come sooner than you imagine.

PART FOUR
KEEPING ON

An object in motion tends to stay in motion. That's our goal here — motion. And not just any kind of motion: Intentional, grounded, and aligned motion to support your highest path. There will be bumps and it will be uncomfortable at times. The more you embrace discomfort and feel okay in it, the more you'll grow as a writer and as a person. Buckle up and enjoy the ride.

CHAPTER 20
YOUR BODY OF WORK

In Chapter 13 we talked about your charcuterie board of content. If you're worried your content, books, and blog posts all read like a mishmash of topics, I invite you to think about everything you write about as a component that goes on one of these tastebud adventures on a wooden plank.

The tastes of the charcuterie board are delicious when enjoyed alone and even better when paired together. And with a delightfully curated presentation, it's also a feast for your eyes.

Applying the charcuterie concept to your writing, each of your blog posts, courses, and books are nourishing and helpful on its own. When enjoyed one after another with a small taste from all the other accompanying content — the experience is even better.

Your group programs paired with your weekly emails.

Your books paired with your newsletter.

Your social media captions paired with your poetry.

Your podcast paired with your workshops.

This is why organizing your content into buckets, or a

handful of key themes, will help your work appear as a charcuterie board. You wouldn't drop mashed potatoes, Brussels sprouts, or spaghetti on your board. It wouldn't fit.

And now, if you're wondering how many themes you have or how even to begin organizing your body of work, here are some ways to figure them out.

Remember that each piece of writing you create is not for everyone. Think about the writers you enjoy — do you absolutely love every bit of their work? Maybe. But chances are that you enjoy some pieces more than others.

Just like the plant-based eater at your party, they're not going to be mad if there's prosciutto on your plate — they'll just eat the things they prefer.

1. Scan your existing writing.

Look across everything you've ever written. If you had to put all the topics into categories, where would they naturally fit? Then, consider your list of groups and think about combining or removing some if there are too many. Are there some topics you no longer write about? You can let those live on the internet and write about things you're most interested in now. If you notice you have a single theme, that's great too. You can absolutely stick to one subject or add more if you feel inspired in the months and years ahead.

2. Consider what you want to be known for.

How do you want people to remember you? Do you want them to remember you for your ability to tell a story and apply a life lesson? Do you want to be known for your no-BS talk? What subject matter do you want readers to associate with your name? Do you want to be a poet who cooks? A romance writer who's also a kickass marketer?

3. Consider what you could talk about all day long.

When you talk about something, and it brings you an inner feeling of excitement and enthusiasm, that right there is magic — follow it. Remember, what feels good to you to create feels good to your readers. List out all the topics that make you feel antsy with anticipation. Subjects so good that you can't wait to share what you know.

4. What do people always ask for your advice on?

If people constantly ask you for cooking advice and you're a life coach, you may want to keep those topics to a minimum. When you notice you're giving the same advice repeatedly, you've got a gift right there. That's the magic sauce you can serve to your audience.

Intuitive Writing Tip

Uncouple the idea that everything you write needs to make money. Some writing can (and should) be for fun or for helping others. Let your art be art without putting pressure on it to do something for you — like make you famous or rake in a million bucks.

5. Write out your list of themes — maybe you have one, three, or even six.

Review each topic on the list. Do you enjoy and want to continue talking about these topics? If not, go ahead and strike some. Maybe what you remove from your blog content is what you'll share in your books. And if you do love these topics, now you have some boundaries to help you brainstorm.

Having boundaries (themes) for your brainstorming and creative projects will give you walls to create within. While many of us might assume that creative people need wide-open spaces to write, I can tell you from working with many kinds of makers and being a creative myself that without a container to create in, I can find myself stuck, procrastinating, and even overthinking.

Give me a nice charcuterie board, and I'll know what to fill it with. Give me a teacup, and I know what to put inside. Pass me a molcajete, and I'm going to make guacamole.

What to do with old pieces of writing that might feel cringey.

When I look back to the mini-book I published in 2015 and my early blog posts from 2012, my instinct is to delete them. I love the newer stuff so much more!

Instead, I leave most of my old writing right there and may revisit and make updates from time to time. It's there for a purpose. Yes, that may no longer be what I write about or even believe, but I want it up there because it all served a purpose in the moment. If people find my old writing and resonate with those ideas, not my new ones, who am I to tell them not to like them?

JOURNAL PROMPTS

1. What do you want to be known for?

2. What do you resist writing about, but are called to repeatedly?
3. What would you love to create if it didn't need to "fit" into your charcuterie board of writing?
4. What kind of writing do you deem "fun"?

CHAPTER 21
JUMPSTARTING & CREATING MOMENTUM

Starting is easy and finishing is hard.

Finishing is hard and starting is easy.

Starting is easy and finishing is easy.

You choose.

I hear from many clients and peers that no matter how many blog posts or books they've written, finishing is often a challenge. These writers all have one thing in common: they're really good at what they do — but they just can't finish a damn thing.

Finishing is awesome. The sense of accomplishment from setting out to hit a goal and getting it done is like nothing else.

In 2015 I had big itches to write a book. I had a handful of ideas, a full-time corporate job with a three-hour round trip commute, two young kids, and was just getting started with my copywriting business. I was in my head thinking I could just roll ideas around in my brain to make things happen. Spoiler — that strategy doesn't work.

A writer I'd followed back then was hosting a small book writing event. An event where we'd focus on getting started on a tiny piece of work. Once you complete a small piece of work, it's easier to go bigger from there, instead of going from zero to five-hundred-page novel. It was a one-day event happening in Portland, Oregon. The event ticket was $500 and would require a two-night hotel stay, airfare from Chicago, food, and making sure hubby's work schedule aligned for getting the kids from school.

I spent weeks thinking about it. So much thinking that I grew tired of it. I worried that it would cost too much money (the total investment would have been all-in around $1,000). I worried about taking time away from my family and that it was going to be too much energy to travel two time zones over just to write a little book.

The afternoon I made the decision, I was sitting in my backyard in our Chicago suburb home, a May afternoon with the early spring sun warming my face through the budding oak trees, and I thought, *What if I don't go?*

Will I regret this decision in ten years if I stay home and maintain the status quo? At the time, I was thirty-five. Would I regret not going at forty-five? Sure as shit would. Sitting with these important questions gave me the confirmation I needed.

I quickly started taking action and made it happen. Signed up for the book writing event, bought my plane ticket, and booked a hotel.

That weekend event kicked off my enthusiasm — an important state for starting and finishing a writing project. Before the writing workshop started, I knew that I had to choose a book writing project. Like many creatives, I had a handful of projects I was considering.

I decided to write a mini-book, *Unfussy Mom: Simplifying Your Life, Staying Sane, and Working Like a Boss.* At that time in my life, I was still full time in my corporate career and just getting started with freelance writing.

That book became my top priority. I focused on writing

and editing that book over the months that followed. The workshop was in July, and I published it by mid-September. Now, it wasn't that I was writing every day, all the time. I found lots of cracks in my day where I could fit in writing. It had me up at 5:00 a.m. writing before the kids would get up — on the train during my commute to and from my corporate job, during lunches, evenings, and weekends. The result was a fifty-page mini-book that I listed on Amazon.

Sure, the subtitle and the contents of that book make me cringe today — and I secretly hope that no one reads it until I make revisions — but writing that mini-book was an important first step. It needed to happen before I could write the next book.

That little book was proof to my brain that I could do it.

That eight-hour book writing event and $1,000 total investment turned out to be one of the best investments I've ever made in myself. I don't think I made even close to that investment back on sales of that first book, but it doesn't matter. It gave me the push I needed to get going — and *finish* my writing project. My first "big" writing project was now complete. What would be possible now?

The beautiful part about finishing writing projects? *Momentum.* By starting and finishing writing projects, you'll get more done. More finished writing projects, more checkmarks on your to-do list, and more growth.

It's important to note that "more" finished projects just for the sake of finishing something isn't the goal. We want to write the things on our hearts — writing what needs to come out and sharing ourselves with the world.

If you've been in a dry spell when it comes to completion, try a small writing project to give your brain a quick win for momentum.

You might be surprised how much you can accomplish in a

day. Here are twenty-five smallish writing projects you can start and finish in the next twenty-four hours. Choose one or a few and prepare to feel accomplished.

1. A three-hundred-word blog post
2. A social post to go with a picture you snapped recently with a short story of what happened
3. An update to your social media bio
4. A thank you note to someone who has helped you out
5. An email newsletter based on your last blog post
6. A mini sales page
7. An email pitch for a podcast you'd love to be on
8. An Amazon book review for a book you loved
9. A resource list of your top five go-to industry experts
10. A roundup of your ten favorite blog posts
11. A list of the books that changed your life
12. A description of your morning routine
13. A fictional story based on a favorite piece of art
14. A poem about one of your favorite things—chocolate, potatoes, dragon fruit
15. A welcome letter for new clients working with you
16. A personal email welcoming your new email subscribers
17. A "see you later" letter when you're wrapped up with a client project
18. Your can't-live-without business tools or software
19. A letter to your mom, dad, partner, kid, friend, or even a stranger
20. A list of things you're grateful for today
21. A list of twenty-five things you loved doing as a kid
22. Your email signature

23. A letter to yourself in the future — one year, five years, or ten years from now
24. An outline or visual map for a book you've been meaning to write
25. A few of your theme words for the coming month or year

As you read these, you may have been nodding along. Uh-huh. And chances are you could write a handful of these in one day or even two of them in the next hour.

Start something. Finish something. Choose one of these items, put this book down now, and start and finish a small project.

WRITING CHALLENGES

A writing challenge can be a great way to strengthen your writing habits and write a lot of words. My books are in the world because of NaNoWriMo.

In July 1999 writer Chris Baty decided to wrangle twenty-one of his friends, and if they wrote 50,000 words or more, they'd earn the title "winner." That inaugural year, only six of the twenty-one writers hit the goal.

The following year, the challenge was moved from July to November "to more fully take advantage of the miserable weather." This is, of course, relative to where you live and your definition of "miserable weather."

NaNoWriMo is now a donation-powered 501(c)(3) nonprofit with a mission to make the world a better, more creative place through stories. Totally with them there. Their programs also support writing fluency and education and host more than a million writers. They're a big deal in the writing world. Today, participants can track their progress on the NaNoWriMo website.

It's a fantastic way to bolster your writing muscles. If you write daily for thirty days, 50,000 words works out to 1,667 words a day.

If you have a competitive streak, sign up with a few writing buddies and check in each day once you've done your writing. Let me tell you, when you see your fellow writer catching up to your word count, you better believe you're going to hunker down, keep going, and cheer each other on.

Summer camp used to be about all the books you could read, sunburns, and bug bites. Now that I'm a grown-up, summer camp is about writing, especially without Wi-Fi.

Camp NaNoWriMo is like its younger cousin, but happens in April and July each year instead of November — and you get to choose whatever word count goal you like.

Whether you're a ghostwriter, copywriter, author, or business owner who writes books, content, sales copy, website words, and more — the spring or summer months might feel like the perfect time to write — longer days, bare feet, sitting on a rocking chair in the sun.

You can use Camp NaNoWriMo to warm up to the big kahuna in November or simply have fun with it.

In addition to NaNoWriMo, I've explored other writing challenges. Some require you to write a bunch of social media posts to see what sticks and drive long-form content from there, some have you enter your words into their software or website. Each have some great points, but not enough that I wanted to sign up for any others.

I also want to share the flip side of thirty-day writing challenges. I did NaNoWriMo for the first time in 2017 when I successfully drafted my book, *Unfussy Life*. I edited it again a year later and published it three and a half years after that

NaNoWriMo draft. And then, in November 2021, I used NaNoWriMo to draft this book you're reading now.

I've always been a fan of using the challenge to write whatever I wanted. For me, that was nonfiction. I've also used the November daily writing habit to draft a big blog series and write a bunch of new website copy.

There's something magical about surrounding yourself with people rolling up their sleeves and putting their words on a page for a common challenge, all in the name of creativity. You can't help but want to do the same. Everyone lifts each other up and encourages each other. (Just one more reason why my writing community is such a special place.)

Sure, I "won" NaNoWriMo every time as I crossed the 50,000-word finish line. There was just one big problem: every time I finished, I was fucking exhausted.

After pumping out at least 1,667 words every day for a month, I fell into the kind of tiredness that would put most people in burnout. I have a ton of creative energy and I love my work so burnout has never really been a story for me, but I felt like I needed to take at least a month off from writing before jumping back in to play with edits.

It's a significant effort to write 1,667 words a day. Especially when I'm doing it while running a growing copywriting and coaching business with a full client load, staying creative, writing and editing for other businesses, looking after myself with good food and movement, and let's not forget driving my kids around so they can live their best lives.

My 50,000-word draft, by the way, was a complete SFD that required many edits and at least one complete rewrite. This brings up something else I hear along among the writing community. The problem with cramming 50,000 words into thirty days is that most of the writing is junk.

Intuitive Writing Tip
Intense writing challenges focus on quantity – not quality.

That lack of quality may be fine for many creatives. Thanks to NaNoWriMo, I wrote two books. And only by taking action did I see there could be another, gentler way to get to the finish line — whether the finish line is a sustainable writing habit or 50,000 words.

The time it took me to draft this book was insignificant compared to my first. I hit my word count goal in under an hour every day while writing with my community — proving that just about anyone can find the time to write a book. Revisions, which come later, take much more time and energy.

Craving a more feminine and flexible approach to writing, I wanted to approach the editing of this book differently.

Learning about the moon and menstrual cycles several years ago was an aha moment. As we chatted about in Chapter 16, a woman's energy is different every day, just like the moon.

A female's energy is different at every stage of the menstrual cycle, which is why, if you have a menstrual cycle and you've participated (or attempted to participate) in a NaNoWriMo challenge, you might have found the words flowed on some days while others on you were too tired to lift a pen. Or maybe you noticed you had too much energy to sit your butt down and write, or you were simply unsure about what to say and feeling the need to go inward.

When we show up to the page and every day looks different than the day before, it's easy to judge ourselves. We wish we could be that fast and flowy writer every day when really, that's just not how we're built. It's normal and okay to feel different each day we sit down to write.

You might have also seen some male entrepreneurs talk

about their daily writing habits. Often kid- and partner-free, they talk about getting up every day at 5:00 a.m., running five miles, downing poached eggs topped with avocado and bacon fat, washing that down with black coffee, then retiring to their office where they write for four uninterrupted hours. And they do this every day. Male hormones are built for this kind of work. Female hormones aren't. There's nothing wrong with this. It's something to become aware of so that wherever your hormones are or the moon phase is, you know that writing can look different for you every day — something awesome you can embrace.

In the past few years, I've hosted a NaNoWriMo challenge inside my writing community. We had a few "rules" every time:

1. Choose your own word count goal
2. Or, instead of a word count goal, choose a writing streak goal — like write for fifteen days out of the month
3. Write whatever the hell you want — a book, blog posts, website copy, podcast notes, a TED Talk, or a combination of items

The goal of NaNoWriMo is to get people into a consistent writing habit. But instead of getting creatives into a habit, I saw it burning people out. I've seen my clients quit halfway through, not start at all, keep a sporadic schedule, and not sink into that new writing routine that they so craved.

I watch the challenge leave many people feeling like failures. But it's not their fault. The push energy isn't for everyone. NaNoWriMo is masculine in its energy — same word count goal every day. Or you could write 50,000 words during the waxing moon for a more feminine approach, but only if the words flow. I decided to explore a more feminine and freer approach.

Inside my writing community in the fall of 2022, we took a fresh approach to writing to nurture our inner writers and potentially change our relationship to writing for the better.

We began at an October new moon and ended at the next new moon in November — lasting roughly twenty-nine days.

Here's how it went:

- We decided our intentions for writing and planted seeds for what we'd create
- We wrote however many words we wanted on whatever writing project(s) we chose
- We pushed ourselves as far as we needed — there was no competition with others, only ourselves

Intuitive Writing Tip

If you try a writing challenge and it feels like it's not for you – throw out the rules and create your own challenge.

The result?

People enjoyed the process. Members reported it felt effortless and a lot more intuitive, like they made slow, steady, and sustainable progress. They finished works in progress, found more ease, wrote several SFDs for blog posts, and got closer to finishing books. I finished a complete round of revisions on this book you're reading now.

Overall, a huge success. It changed how many people felt about writing and showed them how it's less of a daunting, scary task, and more like a fun, relaxing, and easy process.

Resulting in them being able to kick off a long-term, nurturing writing habit.

WRITING RETREATS

The week before the shit hit the fan in 2020, I went on a peer-led writing retreat. In hindsight, I'm sure glad we prioritized that writing event and made it happen.

There are a lot of in-person writing retreats for fiction writers but not many (that I'm aware of) for business owners who write, so . . . I made my own.

Just like it probably is for you, getting *my* writing done is often a challenge. In order to focus at the retreat, I got as much work done for my one-on-one copywriting clients as I could in advance, but I still had some client work to do while I was away.

For me, the draw of a retreat is escaping the familiarity and duties that come with a household — kids, husband, dogs, school, cooking, tidying, sports, shopping. There's much to be said for changing up your scenery, queuing up your out-of-office signature, and putting your head down to work.

Two friends and I traveled to Philly. It was within driving distance of two of us, and the third was willing to get on a plane. This made it easy. We rented a spacious short-term condo with enough bedrooms (and bathrooms) for each of us, plus a great writing table — this and walking distance to restaurants were our top retreat factors.

Doing a working retreat in a city or small town is great for a few reasons: there's no need to rent a car; you can walk to plenty of places (fresh air helps the writing!); there are great spots nearby to eat, so no cooking is required. And you get to explore a city — built-in inspiration. Writing in a beach house, mountain cabin, or on a train trip is also highly recommended.

We were all planning on writing a series of blog sequences that would live on our websites. To prepare, we had some materials to review in advance, and we had two calls for around ninety minutes each to discuss our writing plans, outlines, and even some of the language. Meeting in advance was key to getting organized and keeping everyone on track.

A week before our retreat, I was worried that I wouldn't be far enough along, as one friend had a pretty solid draft already. I was nervous that I wouldn't be able to catch up. All I had was a super rough, two-page bulleted outline. I hoped that getting into retreat mode would help with motivation and inspiration (it did).

We were together from Tuesday afternoon to Friday afternoon. Tuesday was mainly our travel day — meaning we were all tired and not very sharp (speaking mostly for myself). Tuesday afternoon, we gathered at a café while waiting for check-in to finish some work that would have distracted us from writing the next few days. That evening, instead of pushing, we enjoyed a nice dinner and made our plan for the rest of the week.

The rest of the days mostly looked like this (with some variations for each of us):

- **5:00 a.m.** Wake up and work out — no alarm, my body was just ready.
- **6:00 a.m.** Shower and get dressed. I shower and put makeup on every day to prepare for work at home, so this was no different. I was getting ready for my workday.
- **7:00 a.m.** Coffee, respond to emails, check in on projects.

- **8:00–11:00 a.m.** Writing. We wrote in twenty-five minute (Pomodoro) increments with five minute breaks in between. Normally, I work for fifty to sixty minute sprints, so I was worried that twenty-five minutes wouldn't be enough. There were times when I wanted to keep going and others when I heard the timer ding and bolted out of my chair, grateful that twenty-five minutes was over. Breaks were times to pee, snack, stretch, squat, and reset for the next sprint. Hearing the timer go off, letting me know it was time to jump back in again, helped me get back to work even if I was resistant.
- **11:00 a.m.–12:00 p.m.** Lunch. As in, going outside, getting fresh air, and eating plenty of vegetables. And also, in my case, a few pistachio macarons.
- **12:00–12:30 p.m.** Discussing where we were stuck, gut-checking ideas, confirming our writing direction, and brainstorming.
- **1:00–4:00 p.m.** Writing. The afternoon writing sessions were the toughest for me. Normally, I schedule meetings for weekday afternoons, so I'm not used to doing much focused work after lunch. Having two others with me at the writing table, and the Pomodoro clicking, dinging, and buzzing, made it easier. Thinking of my writing time broken into twenty-five-minute chunks made it feel doable. I can do anything for twenty-five minutes! Well, except a plank, but you know what I mean.
- **5:00–7:00 p.m.** Fresh air, walking, and creative well refilling. Whether that was strolling through an art gallery, walking around looking at historic

buildings, churches, and sculptures — it was a brain break.

- **7:00–8:30 p.m.** Dinner. Naturally, we'd end up talking about our work, which led to life, family, and all the things business friends talk about.
- **9:00–10:00 p.m.** Relax, unwind, then bed.

I didn't have a word count goal going into the retreat, but I had about six ideas bulleted out that I needed to flesh out. I guessed that each of the six ideas would be roughly the length of a blog post. It turns out I was right.

- After day one, hour one, I had written 3,557 words (which counted the bullets I had outlined ahead of time). My most productive session!
- By the end of day one, I had 4,700 words.
- By 10:00 a.m. on day two, I had 5,680 words. And I spent much of the second day revisiting what I wrote on day one, which meant tweaking and adding stuff.
- By 11:00 a.m. (lunchtime), I had 6,231 words.
- On day three, I had a three-hour writing marathon in the middle of the day for my community (which meant they were writing and I was coaching) and had to scoot out early to get to my son's playoff hockey game, so I didn't write as much as I thought I would.
- Total three-day writing time for my business: eleven hours.
- Total new words for my business: 8,200 words.

When I first saw the total word count and time invested for

three days, my ego wanted to feel crappy about it — *I should have prepared more, pushed harder, and written more.*

But I stopped that mind chatter. I did more than enough. At this time, I wasn't yet aligning my writing activities with nature's rhythms. We had some great conversations, and I had to think through some business decisions as these came up in my writing. And there were 8,200 words to use in my business that didn't exist before.

Here's an estimated breakdown of my total costs:

- Airbnb for three nights (my portion): $260
- Gas: $30
- Parking: $100
- Lunches and dinners: $400 (this was the highest because I like food and picked up the tab for at least one dinner)

Total cost: $790.

You could do it for much more or much less. Travel costs were low, and food costs were relatively higher.

My biggest worry going into this writing retreat: If I was investing all this time and energy in this trip, I wanted to be sure I'd get more writing done than I would have at home.

Since I didn't plan much in advance, I worried that I'd have too much client work to do or that I wouldn't feel inspired, clear, or even have the stamina to write anything useful. Next time, I'll plan it further in advance and make sure to block my calendar, so I have complete focus.

One of us didn't write for the specific project we were working on at all on day one — and that's okay.

After our second Pomodoro sprint, as I was pouring a third

cup of coffee (the cups were tiny), one friend looked up from her laptop and said, "I'm not writing what I'm supposed to."

Without missing a beat, I replied, "That's okay." Because it *is* okay. She was writing *something* — that's the important part. She was journaling, emailing, and doing other writing.

It was so powerful to see living proof that my belief that writer's block is BS was accurate. She had some stuff to sort out in her mind and heart before she could get to her intended project.

By the afternoon, she was ready to work on her project, and by day two, she wrote like an intuitive MOFO.

I hope this inspires you to create a little writing retreat of your own — to start your website, a book, a screenplay, a few months of blog content, a bunch of poems, or whatever it is you want to write.

Extended vacations can turn into a writing retreat. I've kick-started lots of projects on planes sans Wi-Fi. You'll love how Mairéad, a writing community member, turned travel into a daily writing habit.

> Before 2020, we used to travel for months from Ireland to mainland Europe in our camper van. I wrote a blog post most days. I cannot understand where I found the time. Travel in a van has lots of extra chores because it's not connected to water or electricity, it has no dishwasher or washing machine, and on damp days there's no suitable place to hang your wet clothes. It can get very uncomfortable.
>
> At the time, I worked part-time doing remote bookkeeping, and yet, I had the time to write every day.
>
> It turns out that habits are magic. I always

> started writing on the first day of our trip even as we waited for the ferry to France. That seemingly small habit seemed to spark the daily habit.
>
> And because I needed to write about *something,* another habit powered up — the one that made me notice things. That weird bridge, the fog in the valley, a river bank as a border between two languages — and the disconnect when you can't communicate in said language. The way they check your bags on the way into a shop, the tiny cups of coffee, the kindness of strangers, and even the smell of the campsite toilet block (!).
>
> Every tiny experience held inspiration. I took it and wrote.
>
> And then I stopped. Every time we got off the ferry in Ireland, I fecking stopped! I only just realized, the ferry home powered up the *stop writing* habit.
>
> Habits are magic, including the ones you don't want.

Now, Mairéad is creating new habits at home to support her ongoing daily writing.

WRITING MARATHONS & BATCHING

All those things you want to write can start to pile up. Then there's the updating — for your bio, your blog, your sales page for your next launch. There are sales emails, book promos, refreshing your nurture sequence, follow-up emails. The list of writing tasks feels never-ending.

I get it. It can be hard to make the time to write when you have so much already going on. I'm guessing that right now, at this moment, you have at least a handful of projects you've been meaning to work on for ages and haven't gotten to them.

These writing projects can often feel like extra work. And then they slide down your to-do list because they don't feel urgent. Or worse, they all feel urgent, and you're stuck feeling overwhelmed.

Remember to keep managing your state.

Consider this: What's possible for you when you write those things you've been putting off? Imagine what new doors could open.

Yes, building your body of work matters. Your work in the world is important and deserves a slice of time in your daily pie. Perhaps a bigger slice than you've been dishing up.

The idea of a writing marathon happened when I was contracted as a copywriting coach in an online business-building program. One year, the business owner added these things called "copywriting marathons" as a sign-up bonus for clients. A few weeks into the program, I asked, "What are these writing marathons, and do you need help with these?"

She was happy to delegate. "I have no idea what they are. Can you come up with something and run with it?"

I was intrigued. As I started shaping out what a writing marathon would look like, I started seeing huge possibilities. I asked her if she was okay if I used them in my business. She happily approved, and I hosted a few writing marathons. At the time, they were four hours, which I found exhausting because I was the copywriting coach during the writing marathons, and whenever anyone had questions, I'd talk stuff through. Some were so action-packed that I was coaching, screen sharing, and speaking for four hours straight — except for the breaks I scheduled in.

I hosted my first writing marathon in 2018, and now they're a staple in my coaching community and courses. During marathons, people focus on one writing task or group a bunch of similar tasks. Batch writing is a great way to quickly write a lot of content. And if you post to your blog or email your newsletter subscribers once a week, all you'll need to do is review, edit, and post when it's time to publish. When you spend a few focused hours on a similar task, you can go deeper than if you were bouncing around from task to task.

Through hosting hundreds of sessions with all kinds of business owners, I discovered that two to three hours was the perfect length of time, with a great balance of pushing to finish and still feeling energized and excited at the end.

People are often shocked at how much they can crank out in that time. Here are some examples of what some folks accomplish in just one sitting:

- 2,500 words in a draft sales page
- Two months' worth of content in SFD form
- Three blog posts, an email newsletter, and a social media bio
- A brand new about page
- A sales page and an email for a brand new offer
- A book chapter or two

Batching your writing sessions is a fantastic way to get momentum. And that momentum can keep you going to write more. You may even unlock some more ideas that were bouncing around in your brain.

Want to host your own batch writing marathon? Here's how you might go about it.

1. Pick a date and mark it on the calendar.

Choose a date where you'll have no interruptions and

based on what day of the week you find it easiest to focus on your work. Putting yourself and your project first is an act of self-care. Your writing marathon date is non-negotiable. Treat it like your sister's wedding or an appointment with your hairdresser. Review Chapter 16 on writing with nature's rhythms and choose what days or weeks will be best for your marathon.

2. Plan your rest period.

After your writing marathon, you'll need to rest. Plan for a day off, a creative outing to fill the well, or a light day of work. If you feel compelled to write from all the momentum you've built up, by all means — go for it! This is why it might be best to schedule your writing marathon on a Friday or Saturday so you can easily unplug and take the next day off to let your brain recharge.

3. Choose your flavor of marathon.

Consider different kinds of marathons for what you're working on — one for straight-up immersing yourself in the writing flow, for brainstorming, for journaling and reflection, for editing, for formatting, or for gathering social captions. And then know that when you arrive at your marathon, you might change your mind and want to work on something else. Or perhaps you'll get started with journaling, and then you're so wildly inspired that you want to jump into writing something new.

4. Block two to three hours.

If you've never written for more than an hour at a time, start with an hour. If you haven't written anything longer than a social post in ages, consider writing for just twenty-five minutes and then build onto your writing stretch over time. If you're a seasoned writing marathon pro, you might be able to handle more, and you could block an entire day. I still recommend lots of stretch breaks.

5. Plan your writing session.

If you were running in a marathon, you'd carefully plan your food, drink, clothes, and shoes, and curate a running playlist. All these components are essential for planning your writing marathon too. A week before your writing date, plan out what you'll write. You might craft some blog headlines in advance, choose a few book sections, or determine another writing goal like drafting a year's worth of social posts (I've seen it done before!). Just like running a race, you want to aim for something. When I ran my first half marathon, my goal was "don't die," and I'm pleased to report I prevailed.

Feel free to start with easy-to-hit goals (like don't die), and then as you jump into more marathons, start setting bigger goals to push yourself further out of your comfort zone.

6. Decide where to write.

If you're feeling fancy, you could check into a nearby luxurious hotel or house sit for a friend, where you can skip the distractions and just write. It could also be your dining room, office, co-working space, or coffee shop. Choose a place and make arrangements if needed. If you've ever gotten into the writing flow on a plane at forty thousand feet, you know there's some magic up there. I've seen my peers writing on planes, trains, and car trips, even booking some of those trips just to get some writing out.

7. Curate a playlist.

If you enjoy writing along to music, make a playlist just for your writing session. This is also wonderful because when you cue it up, it's a reminder for your brain that you're about to begin writing. Find a writing playlist in the resources.

8. Set your expectations.

Know that you might set out to write blog posts and feel the pull to write a new sales page for your offer. Follow those hunches. Aim for writing quickly — not for perfectly polished prose with impeccable grammar. I encourage you to embrace the SFD from Chapter 2 here if you haven't already. Focus your editing on an editing marathon to stay in the flow of creating, or break the writing session in half and write the first half, take a break and then edit in the final half.

9. Get your documents ready.

Whether you're getting ready to batch write a month of blog content or a single page on your website, set up the documents you'll need. Pop open a fresh document and add your titles or a rough outline if you're feeling inspired. When I was writing this book, I created separate Google Docs for each section, so I didn't have to worry about any tedious logistics when I wanted to focus on creativity.

10. Eat for a marathon.

Eat a solid meal and try not to over-hydrate — running to the bathroom six times during your writing session might be an annoying distraction. Just as if you were running a marathon, you also probably don't want to eat a huge bean burrito beforehand, or anything heavy that'll leave you ready for a nap.

11. Set your writing scene for success.

Thirty minutes or so before your scheduled writing marathon, clear your workspace, keep a notebook handy for inspiration, have enough beverages and snacks within reach, and make sure you've moved your body a little. Perhaps you'll light a candle, put your feet on the floor, close your eyes for a few breaths, and reconnect with your body. Close the three hundred or so browser tabs you have open and get ready to write.

Set a series of timers to remind yourself to take breaks — play with every twenty-five, forty-five or sixty minutes. And during your scheduled break, stand up, go outside and breathe fresh air, or just walk around for five minutes.

12. Decide how you'll feel when you're finished.

Revisit Chapter 9 on planting seeds in your unconscious mind to set yourself up for an aligned co-creation session.

13. Write like an intuitive MOFO.

It's now your scheduled writing time. You've blocked your calendar, removed distractions, have a satisfied belly and a cup of something energizing, and are ready to write. Write quick and dirty on your topic. Don't worry about grammar, spelling, or even sounding remotely clever. Just get all your thoughts onto the page. If you have time left over, revisit your favorite pieces and start editing.

14. Rest immediately post-writing marathon.

You could be completely spent or wildly energized. Either way, try to plan some rest for your brain afterward. A relaxing evening, a bath, or your favorite way to unwind. If you feel compelled to edit what you wrote, by all means, edit away. And if you don't, that's also great. Just let it sit for a few hours, days, or a week and revisit it later.

Pop the Pellegrino! Because you just sat down with intention and cranked out a piece of work — or many pieces of work. And you spent focused time dedicated to something that matters to you. Revel in your badassery and schedule your next writing session while you're riding the good vibes.

Stuck on what to write during your marathon?

Use these writing prompts to get you out of your head and into your body. Write the first thing that comes to mind.

1. I believe . . .
2. I started this project because . . .
3. What lights me up . . .
4. I do this work because . . .
5. When I sit down with a new writing project, I feel . . .
6. I love this work because . . .
7. I could eat this every day for the rest of my life . . .
8. When I'm not working, you'll find me . . .
9. What's one project that has been sitting unfinished for the longest?

WRITING IN COMMUNITY

I've been hosting online community co-writing sessions since 2018. That's an average of five hours a week of community writing time over five years. Add in the fifteen additional hours for writing the SFD of this book, and that's over 1,300 hours of community writing together. That's 1,300 hours of momentum, productivity, and getting writing projects finished and out into the world in community. Depending on when you're reading this book, it could be so much more.

And beyond the writing marathons, in five years, I've also held hundreds of one-on-one writing and strategy feedback sessions.

I tapped my favorite writing community to answer this question for me: What's your favorite part of writing in community?

1. Borrowed momentum.

You know when you're hanging out with people who make you feel so good that you just want to be around them all the time? Members tell me that sometimes they come to a writing session with no clue or even no desire to write anything at all. Then they see everyone else getting down to business, and suddenly their momentum is fired up, and they're off and writing.

2. Feedback.

Some members opt in for coaching so they get feedback on their writing. But they also learn by listening to the feedback others receive. They learn more than they ever realized they needed to know. And the feedback is fast. Writers come to a session with a blank page, and with focused writing time, they can press pause on outside distractions and get the input or encouragement they need to keep moving.

3. Online courses can only take you so far.

Everyone in the community knows they need to do the work to make writing a habit and practice getting better. Sit down, write, publish, tweak, repeat. Alone on your couch in front of your laptop, devouring all the freebies and $199 courses on the planet can only take you so far. Action is the best and most effective way to make progress in your growing business. Intuitive writers know this.

4. Dedicated writing time.

Some members tell me that they only write for their business during our writing sessions. I plan the writing I'm doing in my business and on my books around these sessions. I'll look at the calendar for the upcoming week and jot down what I'll write or edit during those sessions in my paper planner. I prefer to focus on tasks that tap into my most creative energy when writing in the community, which supports the high vibes there.

5. Accountability.

When it's time to sit down and write a blog post or website copy, it can be too easy to click away from your Google Doc and wander off into social media land to procrastinate. When you're on a live call with a bunch of other creatives who are sitting down to focus and do the work, and you're going to report back on what you've accomplished, you can bet that you'll get your writing done.

6. Variety of businesses.

The Intuitive Writing School Community has grown intentionally at an organic pace. It's a community where members are focused on their work and less on *talking* about not writing. Members who have been working on their writing for years are filled with wisdom to help newer members. It's so much better than looking to one leader to provide feedback to everyone. The perspective that comes from the variety of industries and the owners themselves helps give every member a fresh perspective. And it's not something you can get inside of any free online group full of randos and whoever else the group owner lets in. Hearing from a variety of people what they're working on unlocks creativity we didn't know we had.

Sometimes we have to write things that feel uncomfortable. With the diversity of the group, safely discussing some of the snippets while we write together allows us to gain different perspectives before we hit publish, so our words can become even more powerful.

7. Creative containers.

Give creatives wide open space, and it's easy for us to get overwhelmed and clam up. Give us some boundaries, and we know what we can do. The creative container can give writers the support they need to put one word after another.

8. Connection.

Writing can feel lonely. Writing together eases that feeling of *Am I the only one who's having a hard time with this?* Hearing from others that you're not alone can give you enough comfort to keep going and get through it. When everyone is together yet working on their own things — it feels like *team writing*, and everyone supports each other's goals.

9. Group consciousness.

Be mindful of who's leading you in any setting. Do you align with this leader? Do you feel good when they're leading — are they supportive and encouraging? Does your style vibe with theirs? There's something truly magical when a bunch of creatives come together for a common goal. We feel this medicine so strongly when we're all writing together during a call. And some still feel the power and love of the community behind them when they're not logged into a writing session and know there are big-hearted people who share similar challenges and goals and are all working on something important to them. Alone, together, but not lonely.

You're responsible for the energy you show up with. As a community leader, I can feel right away when someone's energy is off — I sense the tension and overwhelm. When that happens, I ask how they're feeling — often, people need a safe space to share. I might suggest a particular kind of writing warm-up. Almost always, when members arrive stressed out to a call, what's behind it is a lack of presence. They're wrapped up in what the writing needs to *do* for them. Like the writing should be getting them more clients, more sales, more money, and it's not happening fast enough. While it's not my role to try to change anyone's state (that's their responsibility), I can hold the space that's serving the community's highest good.

10. Structure.

How much structure do you have in your life? And is that

structure working for you? When you're shopping for a writing community, you might want to look for one that differs from the strategy you're currently running — which applies only if it's not working for you.

A structured writing community might require you to show your work or track your word count in a community forum to help keep you on track. Some expect members to critique each other's work. What kind of structure do they have? Does one person run all the sessions? Are the sessions longer than you'd typically write?

What days of the week and times of day do they normally write? Will that easily fit into your life, or will that be a stretch for you? Do you want an in-person group, or do you prefer to write from home?

Ready to try it for yourself? See if there's a group of people who already meet up to write in your area. If there isn't, you can always create one.

I created the writing community I needed most, and it works for me. And my writing community is the only one I belong to because I give and get what I need and find it profoundly nourishing. We've been virtual since day one, which carried us seamlessly through 2020.

If you aren't ready yet, pay attention to what might be holding you back and evaluate whether those fears are valid. One fear I hear about often is from people who worry their writing could fall short compared to others.

First — never join a group that makes you feel bad. Look at testimonials, or better yet, ask current members about their experiences in the community before joining.

If a group has a trial offer, see if you like it before going all in. Get a sense of how you feel when you're writing there. And before you go running off for feeling shitty — ask yourself if the energy you showed up with was clear and calm.

In The Intuitive Writing School Community, you only share your work if you want to.

A writing community should be supportive and help you write more (not less), and encourage you with where you are in your journey.

USING AI IN YOUR WRITING PROCESS

When Artificial Intelligence (AI) started gaining popularity in writing communities, some people were freaking out. People wonder if AI will replace copywriters, content writers, bloggers, and books.

Yes, AI will replace some needs for these roles and change industries. AI is a machine. As more people use AI for writing, they're training the machine. The output will improve.

AI writing uses natural language processing (NLP) algorithms to generate text. Note that this NLP differs from the NLP (neuro-linguistic programming) I discussed earlier. These algorithms train based on large chunks of text, like books and articles. The algorithms then spit out new text that claims to be unique and creative.

People can train AI in a variety of writing styles. Say you want to train AI to sound like Hemingway. AI will then generate text that reads like Hemingway. It will never replace Hemingway — or you. You can also teach it to write in different genres, such as fiction, nonfiction, or poetry, in whatever style you like.

However, AI-based creative writing is inherently limited. It won't be able to understand the nuances of human language — especially with emotion and the intricacies of storytelling. AI likely won't accurately capture a writer's intent or get the context right.

And the biggest limitation: seeing AI as a convenient tool without taking the time to think about what it's doing. AI algorithms need training, and people willingly hand over their ideas, prompts, and words to train the box.

Another principle to remember when working with AI is that putting garbage in means getting garbage out. The commands you put into the machine matter. It takes time to learn effective prompting.

Search engines are also putting a significant effort into ranking AI-detected work lower in searches. So, outsourcing your blog to AI won't do you any favors with SEO.

Most importantly, AI isn't connected to you, the you with a soul and a connection to God. AI is just a machine.

A client hired me to fix her sales page copy because someone else she'd hired used AI to generate the copy. I've never looked at a client's writing and thought, "This is hopeless," but the AI writing is soulless and flat.

AI will produce predictable — read, monotonous and mediocre — writing. How boring would our world be if all the books, blogs, websites, and art sounded the same? We need original work. AI knows how to dupe plagiarism checkers, but the ideas you get aren't original.

How I write is different from how you write.

The more we willingly hand over our sovereignty to AI, the more we create a bubble that thinks, acts, and writes the same.

Worse, I see people with blocked throat chakras who think they're terrible writers or have nothing to say look to AI as the answer. "I don't need to write anymore — the machine will do it for me! Yay!" Um. No.

By outsourcing your creative work, ideas, and opinions, you're moving further away from your unique, God-given voice. It's important to note that this is different from outsourcing your copy, content, or book writing to a professional. A good professional listens to and tunes into your voice and will bring it through. A writing or editing professional will listen — a lot — and help you speak your truth, write (or edit) the light that's infused into what you're writing, and help you dial up the brilliance.

CHAPTER 22
WRITING & THE REST OF YOUR LIFE

You've hopefully come to see that you don't need to take a sabbatical from your work to write a book. (Though you could, and if you want to — hey, go for it.)

If you run a business, you know that many things need your attention — your business backend, clients, systems, marketing, accounting, networking. Even if you have a 9-to-5, you've got a full schedule. Add a family and a life, and you might be watching that book idea (or blog, sales sequence, or website copy) slip further away.

You can write for work and personally, *and* have a life — a really freaking fantastic life too. In fact, I encourage you to have a life when you're writing — having a life will make you a better human and writer.

I love getting ideas and inspiration from all the other areas of my life. If it's just you and your laptop, writing ends up being a lonely adventure. No wonder so many people actively resist it.

Without travel, fun, friends, community, and experiences, writing feels flat. The fuller my life is, the more ideas, flow, and inspiration I enjoy. Yes, that also means there may be less time, and so, when it comes to writing, I make the time.

My friend Helene drafted and edited her novel in a year. When a book keeps nudging you, you have no choice but to make the time for writing and fit it into your life.

Here's Helene's story.

> “From my earliest memories in school, I always thought I'd love to be a writer. I didn't know what that meant. All I knew was that I'd love to write. Writing always felt extremely natural to me. The further into adulthood I got, the more I thought my writing would look like a nonfiction business book. And then it started to morph — I got the nudge to try novel writing. I knew that my grandparents on my dad's side of the family had an interesting history of immigrating to the US from Poland. It feels really close to me. There was always this little niggle that there might be something there.
>
> Then I had a baby. A few months postpartum, I had a wave of crystal-clear clarity that there was something to the story of my great-grandmother and how she came to the US in the early 1900s, had her babies, and then took them back to Poland.
>
> I felt into her story. Here I was, holding this three-month-old baby in my arms (like all day long) and imagining myself in her shoes and returning to the country I was born in. I wondered how that would even be a possibility. She was so little. Moving to the US, having your babies, and then returning to Poland — those

babies are US citizens. I pondered what that then ultimately does for a legacy and a family. It's so emotional. And I'm here now, living the life that I live.

This question "what would that be like?" inspired the novel that would come out, but my great-grandmother's life didn't necessarily inspire the story because I researched, and the story coming through was something different.

I went back to my journal entries from a year earlier, and what I saw prompted the rest. All those entries had the theme, "All I want to do is write."

Reading these, my mind swirled. I didn't know how to get started. I thought that maybe I should talk to somebody about this, talk to someone who writes. Or maybe there was a course or a group program I should take.

I was pining for a way to actually do this thing and write. And then, come September 2021, I came across a book writing program and signed up immediately. I started writing my first draft on October 1, 2021.

When I first started drafting my novel (and before I went back to my business post-baby), I was waking up at 6:00 a.m. to write. Because baby K would wake up at 7:00, I wanted to give myself a full hour. I would get up and go downstairs, the coffee maker set to start brewing ahead of time so my coffee would be hot and ready to go.

But I live in this old-ass house and quickly learned that my trip down the creaky steps would wake her up too early. I'd write for five minutes and she'd already be awake. I realized that I'd have to change my plan and stay in my room if I wanted to write this book.

I moved a glider chair into my bedroom, which required rearranging to make it fit. Then, when my alarm would go off at 6:00, I'd get up and head straight to my chair to write. I didn't even pee because if I did, I'd wake the baby. I'd write for a solid fifty minutes, go downstairs and make a bottle, and then go back upstairs and get her.

Now that she's a little older and less sensitive to creaky stairs, we have different routines. These days, my alarm goes off at 5:00. I usually get out of my room around 5:15 to greet my hot cup of coffee, then sit at the dining room table with my MacBook and let myself play. I write for about an hour before getting ready for the day.

Some mornings I dive right into writing or editing. Others, having just woken up from a dream, I feel the need to purge the experience out of my body before I try to write. Even if my busy mind is bouncing around frenetically or I wake up sluggish and don't want to write, I'll open up a blank Google Doc and do some stream-of-consciousness writing first. It's usually only about half a page. Trusting my intuition, I'm often about half a page down when I decide I'm ready to jump into my novel project.

I finished my draft in three months — by December 31, 2021 — and within twelve months of starting, after editing the manuscript twice on

> my own, it was ready for a professional editor's polish and to be sent to agents.
>
> There have been days where I use my entire writing time to just be. I don't force myself to move on to writing or editing after that stream-of-consciousness purge. Probably 95 percent of the time I get to the writing and editing. It doesn't take me that long to get there. But there have been times during phases where I just have to purge it out and release what's going on in my mind before I can produce anything.
>
> Since I've started writing, I've stayed consistent with my approach. I don't force myself to write — ever. With my current phase of life, tending to a baby, I have to do lots of stuff I don't really want to do, but not writing. With writing, it's a definite choice, one that's a whole-hearted *yes*. Like, do you need to drink water and eat every day to sustain your own life? Same goes for writing.

If Helene can do it, you can do it.

By now, I hope you see that there's nothing in the way of your writing. Maybe your life just needs a little rearranging.

Keep filling your creativity well with living, traveling, and connecting. As an online entrepreneur who works (mostly) from home, I know how easy it is to settle into writing from my home office and only venture outside the house for essentials.

This bubble-living can often leave little lived experience for me to talk about, and I may wind up regurgitating things I'm reading online or conversations I'm having with clients.

If we're living in a state where we're constantly consuming and not experiencing, it won't fill us up, and we'll have nothing to write about. Even if you write fiction, your lived experiences give your stories depth and meaning. It's like a bank of mental images that you have to draw upon when you rest your fingers on the keyboard or wield your pen above your notebook.

FAMILY LIFE

When I was writing my mini-book and starting my copywriting business while working a full-time corporate job — both activities that required a lot of writing and staring at a computer screen — I let my family know what I was up to.

Letting your family know that you're not ignoring them and working on a creative project does a few things: It shows them that you're so much more than a wife, husband, partner, friend, parent, caregiver — you're creative. By reading this, you're creative.

When your kids see you creating things that matter to you, it will model someone who cares about their work and their family. A fulfilled parent who's nurturing themselves can better nurture everyone else.

I told the kids what I was working on and shared pieces with them if they were interested. Mostly, they'd say, "That's nice, Mom," which is fine — they're not my ideal audience.

We'll talk about how to handle writing feedback in Chapter 23, but let me remind you now *not* to ask your family for input on your writing. Unless they're your ideal reader or great editors (e.g., my non-ideal-reader husband is a shockingly good editor of my stuff), their opinion might not be helpful. Well-meaning family and friends can steer many people sideways. I've seen business owners sit on their unpublished website copy and blogs because their life partners didn't like the message.

If you're asking for feedback, only invite people you know will be supportive and helpful.

BUSINESS LIFE

Creating some boundaries in your business or work life will help maintain borders around your passion project. Now, this book is both business and passion project. When I was working on this book, I'd pause my email until after my scheduled writing time was finished. I would only dive into business activities when I completed at least thirty minutes of work on my book.

We write in the cracks, and often we need boundaries. Until my thirty minutes a day of writing for *me* are wrapped up — whether for a book project, blog, or sales page, no meetings or client work happen.

Yes, client work makes my business a business, pays the bills, and is another way I serve. I also need to be creative in my own way, getting tuned into my voice to show up even more effectively for my clients. This means I only answer client emails or text messages during my office hours.

Of course, this is my boundary for most days. There are days when life is sprinting at three hundred miles per hour, and I do my writing at the end of the day or not at all.

When I was ignoring my *Unfussy Life* book project, a discussion with my breakthrough coach got me back on track. By doing my writing, I showed my clients that my work mattered. And by doing so, I modeled good boundaries for them — so they could then practice good boundaries.

Intuitive Writing Tip
Whenever you have an opportunity to model the creative life for others – take it. You never know who you might inspire. And you might not even be inspiring them with your words, but encouraging them simply by taking action.

For me, writing is the thing that grows my business, gets my ideas in front of people, connects, and expands — myself, my clients, and in turn, their clients and their families. It's where I share my light with the world. The ripple effect of what one person can do with their words always blows my mind. It's hard to wrap my head around sometimes.

There's never been a better case for enjoying life, business, *and* writing.

SUSTAINING YOUR CREATIVE ENERGY

As an intuitive writer, prioritizing your energy to create is non-negotiable. As you explore your creativity further, you might notice it needs some extra nurturing.

On a quiet week, you'll find me on five hours of Zoom calls — a busy one might see me on twelve. I'm ridiculously intentional with my calendar and know that every meeting on there is one I happily chose. Now that I plan my business and writing activities with nature's rhythms, I schedule those twelve hours of calls in a week where I know my energy will be high.

And even when it's high, I want to keep it high. There's no prize at the end of the week or the end of the year for logging the most hours on Zoom.

Some ideas to honor your sensitive energy:

- If you have regular Zoom calls, unplug your video. I stopped all videos in 2022 and never looked back. Never apologize for being off camera.
- Notice what's going on with your personal energy and nature's rhythm, and start putting boundaries around periods of low energy.
- Plan spacious months — how do you want weeks in the summer to look? Do you want to finish work at 2:00 p.m. every day? Do you want to take Fridays off? Two months off? Block the time today.
- What calls on your calendar could be replaced with an email? A voice message? A walking phone call? Or even canceled completely?

When you're on calls and notice you may be taking on others' energy:

- Wear a bracelet on your left hand (the left receives, and the right gives), and imagine your receiving energy is filtered into the bracelet and not getting into your precious bod. Clean your bracelet by placing it in the sun afterward.
- Hold something in your left hand like a crystal, stress ball, or stone when others are speaking — especially handy if they're ranting, offloading, complaining, or processing. Imagine the object is holding whatever is coming your way, so when your conversation is finished, you can place it down and leave the energy with the object, rather than carry it around or even allow it to infiltrate your energy field. Remember to clean those crystals in the sun or the full moon when they need it.

- Picture an imaginary bucket off to your side (mine is gold) and someone's filling the bucket (a good in-person practice, too, when you encounter an energy vampire). When they're done speaking, lovingly imagine you're handing the bucket back to them so they can process their stuff (it's not yours to process).

During a full day of meetings:

- Light a candle in between, burn a little incense, sage, or palo santo.
- Go outside and put your bare feet on the ground and feel the sun on your face.
- Dance it out like no one's watching.
- Take extra good care of your nutrition with whole foods — fruits, vegetables, nuts, and seeds.

Your energy matters in everything you do. And when we work and live with others, it can be easy for the most sensitive among us to take on others' shit. Which doesn't do us or them any good.

CHAPTER 23
SHARING YOUR WORK

One of the biggest fears my new clients and community members have is sharing their work. They bring instant shame to their work — "This is embarrassing," they often say as they share the link. I have a lot of compassion for those who share their writing with me. And, for the record, I've never once thought, "Yikes, they should be embarrassed."

If there's one thing that freaks out writers the most — it's letting others see their work. Whether you're looking for feedback or not, hesitating to hit publish, or just seeking an outside opinion — hitting send on your writing can be nerve-wracking.

When I sent the SFD of this book to my editor for her initial feedback, I might as well have been hosting a live-streaming session — from my bathtub. I felt naked and afraid. And it was okay. I didn't die. And the very first shitty manuscript of this book looked quite different than it does resting in your hands. That's the magic of embracing feedback and jumping back into your writing like a five-year-old with her glob of modeling clay.

When publishing my first few blog posts, that same fear

crept up too. Most of the time now, I finish it up and fire away — no ruminating, no overthinking.

Why do we writers have this fear — where does it come from?

We can usually trace this fear back to our school days.

Imagine you're in seventh grade English class, thinking you did a great job on your latest essay. You're feeling sassy as the teacher starts passing out the stack of graded papers, anticipating she'll show it off to the class as a mighty fine example. But then she returns your paper to your desk, no eye contact, dropping it face down.

"Oh, she just didn't want me to show off my grade," you think as you lift up a corner to peek, searching for a grade.

If the grade was anything lower than an A+, it gives you the instant sense that you didn't do well enough. You think your work wasn't good enough; *you're* not good enough. You draw all these conclusions in a flash.

The red pen of doom scribbled all over our hard work, with arrows, circles, and X's all over it. Then comes the next writing assignment, and we feel even worse than last time. We start writing and wonder, what's the point? The teacher is going to hate it anyway.

This example might be a walk in the bookstore compared to your experience. I've heard other stories of damage that teachers caused — for example, teachers who hold their students to the same impossible standards they hold themselves to.

Teachers pass down their same rejection wounds onto students, and it's sad.

We internalize that perfectionism is a good thing and we started pointing to it as our weakness in job interviews as a way to stand out.

Take years of this bullshit in the classroom, and when you

start a business and go to publish your website or very first blog post, email newsletter, or social post, it's no wonder you want to crawl into a hole and cry.

The red pen is meant to help us grow and show us where we need to improve. There are certainly shitty, unsympathetic teachers who bruise with comments, but there are some who are truly trying to encourage. For this supportive teacher, the red pen is a good thing.

For every shitty English teacher out there, my optimistic side tells me there are at least three more supportive and encouraging ones whose red pen is meant to improve and stretch you in your writing ability. And perhaps writing coaches like me, who will nudge you to keep writing and share your work over and over.

If you're feeling apprehensive about who you share your work with and when — go slowly. Make sure you find someone you trust.

WHO TO SHARE YOUR DRAFTS WITH

When I host public writing marathons with live copy feedback in a group setting, many people join because they want fresh eyes on some copy they've been overthinking. And it's surprised me how many people email me afterward saying they were too scared to share.

For this purpose, I often ask a few clients and writing community members to come to the public sessions and go first so they can show the new folks that it's a warm, friendly, and supportive space. I'm not your seventh grade English teacher and only use red pens to draw little hearts and butterflies. I can also tell you that I've never seen any piece of writing that was truly hopeless.

Here are some thoughts on who to share your work with:

- In a business mastermind or small friend group with someone who understands you and your audience.
- If you need a first dose of support and unconditional love, then ask a friend or family member who you know will deliver just that before you go down the road of asking for feedback from anyone else.
- Ask a writing coach who you've seen in action online or someone who has come recommended by someone you trust. When receiving a recommendation, ask them how the coach delivered feedback and determine if this is what you're looking for.
- Please be mindful of sharing with people who have something to sell you. I've watched too many tentative business owners drop a link to some writing they decide to share in a Facebook group only to have a bunch of people vying for business tear it apart, thinking they're doing them a service, only to pitch them later.

WHEN TO SHARE & WHEN TO HOLD OFF

When I was writing *Unfussy Life*, I asked for feedback from too many people too soon. I tried to time it with what I thought would be the final review from my editor. It turned out the book would change a lot from that point. This was also before the book decided it wanted to be a memoir. Much of the feedback I received from very early readers was good but didn't end up being useful because I changed the manuscript so much.

That said, I often share snippets of my super shitty first drafts with my writing community — not for feedback but to demonstrate what a true SFD looks like. Mine are so rough they barely make sense.

When you're ready to share, being specific about what kind of feedback you need will save you time down the road. Here are some suggestions on how to ask for feedback:

- When sharing your work, give people boundaries for reviewing your work. Instead of free rein to dish up whatever comments they like with questions such as, "Did you like it?" ask specific questions such as, "Did the theme come through in this section? What was your favorite part? Did any part confuse you?"
- Giving people boundaries for providing feedback makes it easier for them to provide you with feedback that you can apply. It can also head off unhelpful feedback like, "It's great, I love it!" This kind of vague praise can often leave us feeling worse — *Wow, are they lying to make me feel better?*

NAVIGATING & HANDLING FEEDBACK

Okay, so you've gotten some input on your writing. Now it's your responsibility to discern what to pay attention to and what to put aside. Not all feedback is worth listening to. In fact, most isn't — especially feedback of the unsolicited variety.

Here are some helpful filters to run through:

- Was the feedback solicited or unsolicited?
- Do you respect the person who shared this feedback?
- Is there some aspect of the feedback giver's life or business that you admire and want to emulate?

- Do you look to this person for mentoring and advice?
- Where's the feedback coming from? Are they doing their own inner work?
- Could their comments be projections of their own wounding?

When you receive feedback that feels off, sit with that feeling and put it aside until you're ready to explore it. If you determine that the feedback is negative and absolutely not for you, imagine putting their words into a bubble. A bubble that doesn't touch you. It stays outside of you where you can pop it and let it disappear.

It's always up to you to decide what to take and what to leave. You have no obligation to take anyone's feedback. Remember, it's your name on the cover, on the blog, or in the email "from" line — you get to choose.

SHARING YOUR WORK PUBLICLY

Sharing a piece of work for the first time might make you feel a little queasy. Over time, that feeling will lessen. You get to decide how you feel when you hit publish — remember, you can manage your state every step of the way.

There are also three other things it takes to put your work out there:

1. Courage
2. Trust that the work that came through you is perfect
3. Surrender — or not giving a fuck about the outcome

The last one takes longer to cultivate than others. Perhaps

you were born with the not-giving-a-fuck gene — for that, I'm envious. I used to give too many fucks in all the wrong places. I gave fucks to those wounded teachers and managers early in my career. I learned how to write to please them (not to write what felt good to write), and I was good at it. Oh, the thousands of fucks I gave for the thousands of words I wrote in corporate to please someone else.

Too many fucks for the "mockamole" edamame recipe I put out there, and people were all, "What do you have against avocados?" Sheesh, people, I'm just giving edamame some love.

The direct messages telling me I had a typo in a social media post and should be more careful. You know, because I'm a writing coach and people need to take me seriously.

Worrying about how blog posts would be received. Worrying about promoting anything to my email list. Worrying about being judged. Worrying about selling. Worrying about how I'd be perceived for my rates. *Was it too much, not enough? Who am I to charge this much?*

Guess what? You will be judged. And never by people who are as far along or more successful than you. The people judging are the ones still sitting on the proverbial couch, not taking action, not writing books, and not starting businesses.

If you're speaking truth, you will trigger some people. This is a good thing. Triggers show us where we need to look to do more healing. They show us the parts of ourselves that we've been ignoring, stuffing down, or numbing. If something in this book triggered you — you have new information to help you move forward. Just keep moving forward.

Dropping the proving, performing, and people-pleasing habits has helped me get my work out in an authentic, feel-good, and aligned way.

Especially when writing for myself — my books, newsletters, blog posts, and social posts — I write what I'm passionate about at the moment. I create, share, repeat.

When I first started my food blog back in 2012, I triple-checked every word and constantly read them over. And even still, I'd find typos after publishing — almost every single time. I used to feel a sense of panic and rush to fix them as soon as I noticed. Now, if I see a typo, sometimes it's years later.

Business owners are afraid to share their work for a variety of reasons. Be it a combination of the shitty high school teacher, a demanding parent, or a jealous sibling, they're scared their email subscribers will be mad at them for selling something, they won't like a message, or they'll unsubscribe. Make sure you turn notifications off for unsubscribes. You don't need to know when that happens. Trust that every unsubscribe is making way for a more aligned email subscriber in the future.

You have to be okay with rejection to put your work out there. It's part of being seen as an intuitive writer.

Here are a few things that it might help to remember:

Your work isn't you. That's your ego thinking it is. When you're creating from a fully surrendered place, you're co-creating (and, in this case, co-writing) with the Divine. Your work is an extension of you and your energy.

We can all only be shown in our external experiences what's going on in our minds. So when someone hurls some hate at you saying they're offended, know that something is going on within them. It is really only about them and has nothing to do with you, your worth, or your work.

If someone shares that they took great offense to something you created, look around within your life — where have you been offended recently? Maybe that person who was so offended by my mockamole recipe just prepared a dinner his family secretly fed to the dog.

Honestly, I don't have haters. I've only had good and great

client experiences. It comes from knowing that I trust myself. If you encounter a hater, thank them. It means you're doing great sharing your voice authentically. And for every hater, there are probably a dozen people who love your writing.

Keep writing.

Keep sharing.

ON CANCEL CULTURE & HONORING YOUR INTUITIVE WRITING

You've probably witnessed one or more business owners or content creators get taken down — very publicly. Former fans feel like they've been had or take offense at something said — so it triggers feelings of embarrassment, betrayal, and shame, which is really only old wounding showing up.

They gather around this business or the person behind the business and try to ruin every aspect of it — leaving one-star reviews on their books and podcasts, and filling their comment sections on social media with venom. All in a great effort to "cancel" that business or human. The result these snakes in the grass often want to see is a total takedown — they want them to fold their business and go away. But what happens if they fold their business and go away? Think about who goes with them — their family relying on their income, their kids' sports, maybe their employees, and those families' families.

Of course, it isn't to say a business owner should be doing something shitty or shady and profiting from it. You choose where you put your money and can decide whether or not to support these people. By publicly calling out people who trigger you and holding them to the same, or even higher, unreasonable standards that you hold yourself to, you're perpetuating more of the same. And you're giving them energy that you could use for writing.

One more thing: If you've ever sat and watched a shit show cancellation go down from the sidelines, glued to your screen like it's a soap opera, scrolling through the comments, you're not only perpetuating darkness, you're also distracting yourself from the work you're here to do.

I've seen friends and colleagues on both ends of call-out culture. If I see anyone I know going out of their way to call someone out publicly for no good reason, I know they're not aligned for me. If you're following people who call people out, who's to say they're not going to call you out next?

Watching all this kerfuffle go down can be enough to make people close their businesses, never start, or stop sharing their work. Witnessing others' inner children and ego on display can be the trigger that says to your unhealed inner children, *"Don't put your work out there; it's not safe."* But safe from what exactly? Any kind of attention — good, bad, and ugly — is still publicity. As long as you can keep your give-a-fucks to zero, you can take that shitty energy directed toward you and transmute it into growth and expansion.

You have to create what you're called to create. Share your work in the best way that feels good to you. Trust the process and yourself, and write.

And when it comes to deciding when and how to share, make your decision from a place of love, not fear. When you make decisions out of fear, you can only bring more fear.

After that pep talk, I hope you'll share your writing. Someone needs to read it.

NOW THAT YOU'VE PUBLISHED SOMETHING

WoooooοHoooo! I'm raising my bottle of sparkling water to you now for putting yourself out there.

You may be wondering, "Okay, I closed my eyes and hit publish. What do I do now?"

Here are some ideas about how to share your work further so your writing can touch more souls:

1. Share it on the social media accounts you actively use and add a few words around what went into creating it, what inspired your musings, or who needs to read it.
2. Cut and paste the text with a pretty picture directly into a social media account.
3. Email the lovely people who have given you their email addresses and let them know. Make sure you include a few other updates too. Hint: "I blogged" is not an update.
4. Did someone inspire your writing? Send it to them with a quick note, saying, "Hi! Thanks for being awesome. Your thoughts on [smart thing they wrote] inspired me to write this [link to your writing]!"
5. Do you have more to say on this topic? Write a spin-off blog post, create an opt-in to help grow your email list, or write a book about it.
6. Did you receive some thought-provoking comments on social media? Turn this into a blog post, email newsletter, poem, manifesto.
7. Have you written about similar topics? Start writing your book! You'll edit later. For now, just copy and plop that pretty little blog post into a Google Doc.
8. Print it out and frame it.

9. Collect a few of your favorite pieces of writing, send them to a printing company or arrange them in a photo book, and gift them for the holidays
10. Print it out and burn it at your next bonfire. Trust there's more where that came from.
11. Link to previous articles you've written.
12. Read it aloud and send the recording to your email subscribers.
13. In a year, revisit, refresh, and republish it!
14. Add a link to it in your email signature.
15. Add a roundup of links to your latest writing in your next out-of-office autoreply message.

Whenever you share, however you share, do it with love, and do it as often as your heart desires.

CHAPTER 24

GETTING BACK TO WRITING AFTER A CURVEBALL

Life will throw you curveball, fastballs, and many perfect pitches. Sometimes it'll throw you a flaming pile of dog shit. And many times it will delicately drop miracles into your lap too — whether you believe in them or not.

Life is gonna life.

Makers are gonna make.

And writers are gonna write.

Living the intuitive writer's life is messy, beautiful, and delightful. And you're still a writer when you're not writing. You're a writer if you're an entrepreneur writing blog posts. You're a writer if you're a coach and love writing letters, and you're still a writer if you write a moving social media caption. You're a writer if you tell stories, and you're a writer if you send a darn good email.

This is why we write in the cracks. We write to connect. We write to heal. Whether we're writing a little or a lot — we're still writing.

Yet there will be times when you're all in on a project, and life has other plans.

Like when I got so busy with my growing business that I stopped working on my book.

Or the time I had an email newsletter list but didn't create a welcoming nurture sequence until four years after I'd gone full time in my business.

Or the second day of writing this book, receiving the sad news that our old-timer dog had cancer. (Again, here he is, sleeping at my feet while I edit this very section.)

The curveballs will happen — and if continuing to write and perhaps changing your pace is what will work best for you, then do that. Otherwise, let yourself press pause.

There have probably been many times you went into your writing project with the best intentions, pens blazin' and ready to write.

Whether you were hoping to write a book, a bunch of blog posts, your website copy, or an email series promoting your next big thing, maybe one of a few things happened:

You started off feeling good and making progress. You wrote every day for three days, first thing each day, and then something got in the way — (*insert your reason here — the dog got sick, the school was closed, your water heater broke*).

You missed a day, and then two, and three.

Or you wanted to start on Monday morning. You had a plan and even prepared with some new pens and candles to help you get in the writing mood.

Except the night before, you woke up at 2:00 a.m. and couldn't get back to sleep. You lay awake until 6:00 a.m., when your alarm buzzed off your nightstand. *How the hell are you supposed to focus on the responsibilities of your day, let alone write a book when you can barely function without a pot of coffee?*

Whether you started your writing project strong or slept

through the go-time horn, you *can* get back on the horse and cross the finish line with a finished writing project.

If you're reading this in the middle of a writing dry spell, I invite you to look at these ideas for getting back into your writing project as a menu. Choose one that feels exciting and get moving.

1. Instead of a word count goal, consider a writing streak goal.

If you were focusing on hitting a certain number of words, change up your target. Can you write three days a week for the rest of the month? Or could you write for fifteen minutes a day on weekdays? Try to focus less on how long you wrote as long as you dedicated *some* time to writing that day.

2. Start right now — literally.

Don't procrastinate further by finishing the rest of this chapter. Save your spot, set a timer for twenty-five minutes, and write as fast as you can until the timer dings. No editing, judging, thinking, or criticizing. Move on with your day, and do it again tomorrow. Then come back to this chapter.

3. Consider a reward or series of rewards for hitting milestones.

Rewards work! Maybe a bonus like a new notebook when you hit a specific word count — five thousand, ten thousand, or twenty-five thousand words. Or perhaps book a massage or night out to celebrate not only your achievements but also your effort and dedication for a finished product.

4. Move the goalpost further out.

Whatever your writing goal — you chose it in a made-up system of time that doesn't matter. As a tiny speck in the multiverse, consider what meaning your project has. Change your goal to the end of the year (unless you're reading this on December 31), make a plan to write, add the time to your calendar, commit, and do it.

5. Revisit your project.

Consider the underlying reasons why you're not finished with your project yet. Is it a project you've tried to work on before and have struggled with? What's your intention behind the project? Could it be that you're writing something out of fear (a terrible motivator) or from love (the only place to write)? If it's a project you're writing out of necessity — and one that only you can write, put on your big kid pants, place the time on the calendar, and commit. If you're writing something because you feel you have to and there are a dozen other things you'd rather be writing — can you hire help to get someone to write it for you?

Creation is an act of surrender, and the more you can surrender, the easier it is to write.

Surrender is where we find the flow state.

If you can hold yourself accountable to a goal, regardless of its scope, you can know you showed up for yourself in the best way you could — even when life gets in the way.

When you're fully surrendered, all those made-up ideas of why we can't write fall away. There's no writer's block, resistance, or inner critic.

CHAPTER 25
INTUITIVE EDITING TIPS

Yay! You've done a great job with getting the words out, and now you have a new project to tackle: editing. I hope you took the earlier advice and restrained from editing while writing.

Editing is a completely different adventure from writing.

You might find editing easier than writing because the words are already there for you, and you just get to play with them now.

You might find editing harder than writing because this is where perfectionism sneaks in, and you're overthinking every sentence, unsure of grammar rules, and what to change and what to leave alone.

When coming to the page to edit your work and your words feel chaotic and overwhelming, remind yourself of nature. What appears chaotic is really perfect order. Trust that order is in there and it's your job to uncover it. And you will.

When it comes to editing copy for the online world, I ignore most grammar rules. Instead, the goals are writing to connect and to make a clear point. When I'm writing something that will have lots of eyes on it, including strangers' eyes, like a book — I invest in an editor. If you're not a professional editor, hiring help will be the best investment of your money, time, and energy.

For my books, I hire both a professional editor and a proofreader. The editor and proofreader should be different people. If you hire an editor, they may work with a proofreader, so you don't have to worry about it.

When you're hiring for a proofreader or editor, getting personal recommendations is gold. Next, talk to a few people to understand their process. Ask for samples and see if it aligns with your writing. As always, trust your intuition when it comes to who to choose.

If hiring an editor doesn't make sense for your project or budget, find a trusted reader or circle of writers to review your work. Keep in mind you want *helpful* suggestions here.

Editing others' work also makes you a better writer. If you have a few peers with whom you can share your work, consider trading your eyeballs to review each other's projects.

SURRENDER IN THE EDITING PROCESS

We've talked about how to surrender at the page when writing, but what about during editing?

Dawn, a friend and former client, surrendered and trusted Divine timing with her first manuscript. Here's her story.

> “It was a wild experience when I started my first round of edits. I looked at the draft and didn't remember writing it. Of course, there were parts, like, *oh my gosh, what's happening here?* But by and large, I was really impressed with myself — which is a great feeling.
>
> Many times in the editing process, my mind has come up with a plan of how I'll get through

the edits. I booked myself a four-day personal editing retreat. Going into it, I thought, I'm gonna kick off my second round of edits. I'm gonna hammer it out and get so much of it edited – like half of the book. It's gonna be amazing.

That's not what happened. I sat down with my printed manuscript for about four hours on the first day, highlighter and my favorite pen ready to go. I read through the whole thing, making notes, absorbing the story as it was at that point. Then, I didn't touch it for the rest of the retreat. Not once.

It took me a good half a day to be okay with that. I kept thinking, I should be editing, I should be editing, I should be editing. And then, I distinctly remember making myself a fire and trying to edit. But I didn't like the edits that were coming through. That night, I was like, hey, if I edit tomorrow, I edit tomorrow – if I don't, I don't. I didn't edit the rest of that retreat weekend. I didn't pick up edits again for two more months. And I had to be okay with that.

Even though I knew time was ticking, it felt extremely hard, like I was forcing it. And I was not going to force it. I just won't. It's so much better when I don't, even if it's not on the timeline. You know, that egoic timeline I create with my mind.

To finish my edits, I later carved out time each morning. And after a few months, it was ready for a professional editor.

Writing and editing might look different than what you

imagine. Surrender and trust that your experience is exactly what you need.

TIMING YOUR EDITING

Make the most of your energy and the collective energy, and see how your editing flows during the waning moon or the luteal phase of your menstrual cycle — your personal "fall." See if your attention to detail is sharper and if you're catching more typos and spots to improve.

Make sure you've given the writing some space to breathe between letting it out and going back in with a carving knife to shape it into what it wants to be. Give a piece of writing an hour, a week, or a month, and when you revisit it, you may find you'll dive right in and easily make changes.

If resistance is creeping up with editing, you can approach editing with all the same mind tricks as we did with writing. State management, timers, rewards, putting it on the calendar, making a plan are all great ways to get your editing project done.

Even if you hire an editor, you'll want to have a conversation with them, or even ask for a sample edit, to get a good understanding of their style. A writer's worst nightmare is investing hundreds of hours into writing something — a website, a book, something else — only to have an editor change up the entire voice so it doesn't feel like them anymore.

DON'T LOOK FOR YOUR WRITING VOICE – CREATE IT

You create your voice with a blend of writing, reflecting, and editing. I cringe a little when people say they're working to find their voice. I stay away from the idea of finding a voice. Because what would happen if you never found it? You could spend your entire life looking for something. What if you find it and don't actually like it? Then what? Throw in the towel and never write another thing? That's some crazy talk right there.

Bit by bit, over time, as you grow, develop, tune in, you'll see your writing voice is more of a chiseling out. You'll find little nuggets to incorporate into your writing over time. And as you continue consistently showing up to the page, some may fall away. As life is going to life and writers are going to write, you choose the words you put out there.

And then in revision, you can make your voice sparkle. Revision is a chance to layer in more humor, emotion, and texture. You might think that editing is only about grammar and spelling, but it's really about adding more layers of *you*.

For this reason, many people are worried about hiring a copywriter or editor for their big writing project. They're afraid they're going to lose themselves.

There's no way to lose your voice if you make sure you like the one you have already. This means you'll practice writing—over and over. When working with editors on my books, I appreciate all the suggestions and options. And if an editor makes a decision I disagree with, I get to choose. Also, a good editor only wants your voice to shine and ideally will help that happen. A great editor or writing coach will show you how to hone your voice.

If you hire an editor, copywriter, or ghostwriter, check out samples of their work. Do they all sound the same? Or can you clearly discern each person's unique voice in there?

You're probably going to be editing most of your writing yourself. I wrote and edited my website copy, every blog post, and email until late in 2021, when I hired some editing help for a short time. I later came to realize that the editor was editing my voice out, so I returned to doing my own editing for blog content.

I do multiple rounds of editing on my books with my editor. We'd pass the whole piece back and forth, reviewing comments and addressing changes.

I see many people hiring a writing or editing professional because they think they don't have the time. A word of caution: Even if you hire it out, you're still going to have a significant time investment on your hands.

Here are my favorite ways to perform a self-review of whatever you're writing. These strategies apply to website copy, emails, social posts, sales letters, books, bios, literally anything you deem necessary.

Get clear on the purpose of your writing piece. Before you dive in with your purple pen (kinder than red), ask yourself:

- Is the purpose of this piece of writing clear? What's the context?
- Do I have all the details I need to refine this or do I need to do some research?
- Do I want my reader to feel a certain way?
- What tone do I want to hone?
- Who's the reader? Is it clear? Think beyond demographics — what are they thinking, feeling, and hoping for in the moment they discover this piece of writing?
- If this is a casual piece of writing, is it conversational? Did I use contractions to make it conversational? (I will => I'll; you have => you've)
- Did I use easy-to-understand words instead of longer or more advanced terms? (Keeping it simple is an act of service for your reader.)
- What grade level of a reader is this writing for?

Intuitive Writing Tip
Using contractions in your writing (I am => I'm; we will =>we'll) is the easiest way to make your writing feel approachable, conversational, and friendly – useful for building trust with your reader.

Once you're clear on the purpose of a piece, you can decide what calls to action (CTAs) you want to include.

- What do I want the reader to do? Is that clear?
- What one action do I want them to take after they read this?
- Do I need CTAs throughout the writing? At the end?
- Can I link to other relevant writing pieces or content within this piece?

Before you hit publish on anything, it's important to give it a final review. Here are my top proofreading tips:

- Put this piece of writing aside for a few hours or a day or more before proofreading.
- Print it out and review it with a pen.
- Read it aloud — would I speak this way? Does my ideal client speak this way?
- Read from bottom to top, one sentence at a time.
- Increase the font to a super-large size so that you scroll through slowly.
- Change the font to give you a new perspective — go from a sans serif font to serif (or reverse).
- Read it on a different device — like a phone or tablet if you typically review on your computer.

- Read in a different location — your couch, outside, the kitchen, or somewhere other than where you wrote it.
- Check to see if you've removed the passive voice as much as possible. (Passive: It was decided. Active: I decided.)
- Run it through spellcheck or a grammar checker.

If you're asking someone else to review the piece, ask these questions:

- How much time do they need?
- What filters are they running it through?
- How can I help them review it for what I'm looking for most?

The final few questions before publication are for you:

- Is this complete?
- Is this ready to share or publish?
- If this was published today, would I be confident it's authentic and accurate?

Every time I sit down to write or edit anything, I aim to do a few things:

Help you write more.

Inspire you to want to write.

Encourage you to go for it.

Remind you that writing can be easy. (*You just gotta do it!*)

Everything I share has a variation of the above goals backing it up. I refuse to write something that doesn't meet those goals just because it's blogging day.

And like me, you probably write from the heart. You give a

shit about your work, your people, your brand, and probably lots of other stuff too — like recycling, choosing the good chocolate, saving the whales, or whatever cause tugs on your heart.

The world needs your helpful, engaging writing. In many of my writing workshops, clients tentatively share their work with me.

"Is it good enough?" they wonder.

Almost always, it's perfect. Perfect in the sense that the intention behind the article is clear and powerful, and the essence is to help, inspire, entertain, or educate. It's not about being perfect in the sense that every comma is in the right place, they're writing in an active voice, or a sentence structure is spot on.

If your heart is in a good place when you sit down to write and you're doing your inner healing work outside of coming to the page, your readers will almost never notice, nor care about the odd typo or funky sentence.

When you're writing something that could be potentially damaging to yourself or others, here are some additional filters I run everything I share publicly thorough, in order:

1. Is it good for me?
2. Is it good for the people I love?
3. Is it good for my community?
4. Is it good for humanity?

The first one is the most important. If it's good for you, that's more than enough reason to move forward. The goal in reviewing this checklist is to make sure you're being helpful.

If a particular story feels unsafe or hard to share, I explore why I'm hesitant to share.

You have permission to hit <publish>, intuitive writer.

Sometimes, people ask me if their blog article is good enough to post. My answer almost every time is, *yes!* We can tweak for hours, but for what? They often hesitate to hit publish because they're worried more about how they'll look to their peers, mentors, and coaches — the people who are *not* their ideal readers.

On the occasion when it's not quite ready to publish, often it's missing some key items — a conclusion, clear message, or call to action — or there are some opportunities to flesh out important details.

Here's your official permission slip. There's a caveat, though; you only get *one* permission slip because you don't really need it, and you can write your own intuitive writer permission slips now.

Your writing will improve if you keep doing it. The more you face the page and make something out of the thoughts swirling in your head, the more you'll continue to strengthen your voice. When you sit down each week and focus deliberately on writing something that your audience craves, you grow your body of work, bit by bit, until you have a dozen articles, then fifty, then hundreds.

COME OUT OF HIDING

But what about when we hover over the <publish> button, afraid to put our words out there?

Hiding your work is your ego talking. As much as we may point to our egos for wanting to be seen, go viral, or experience fame, the opposite is also true. If you're hiding, afraid to put your work and yourself out there, this is also the ego piping up trying to protect you. Give that bugger an elbow to the gut (and make a note to kill that MOFO later), publish, share your work, and carry on with your life. You're ready. Your writing is ready. Get it out there.

If you notice a mistake later, it's okay! We all do it. If it's in social media, depending on the context, you can leave it and move on. If it's on your blog or your website, go ahead and make a quick fix.

Usually, we're the only ones who notice our mistakes.

Keep creating, keep writing, and keep going. Build that body of work!

OUTRO

By this point, hopefully, you've begun to heal your wounds, quiet your mind, fuel your body, and clear what's in the way of your writing,

Now it's time to take what you've learned and make intuitive writing a part of your life. A big part. I invite you to immerse yourself in the intuitive writing life. Just like learning a new language is far more successful when you're living in a foreign country and speaking it every day, immersing yourself in the writing life is a game-changer.

By keeping your writing project at the top of your priority list, you'll consciously and unconsciously be focusing on your topic, which will make creation feel easier.

Even when you're not writing, you'll be thinking about writing. Except now you're coming to the page consistently and getting the words out, so you forgive yourself for not writing. You'll be okay on the days you're not writing because you know there are so many more days that you *are* writing.

You're no longer a dabbler. You're committed to being a channel for your creative project and giving the Divine, God, Source a chance to work through you. While you're going about your day knowing you're making progress on your writing project, you'll start to see synchronicities and messages that support your writing.

Putting your soul's work on the back burner no longer serves you or your writing projects — it's a misuse of your gifts.

You see that writing doesn't have to suck. It doesn't have to be complicated. It doesn't have to hurt or feel like torture. You define what your intuitive writing life looks like.

Writing has become a beautiful complement to the rest of your amazing life. Allowing, surrendering, and showing up to the page.

The more you make peace with the writing process, the more people can share your stories. The more you're connecting with loved ones, friends, and strangers and feeling proud of yourself, the more you can heal through writing.

Start your writing project today. Immerse yourself. Play with it. Finish it, make progress, give fewer fucks about what others think, put your words out there, build your body of work, and keep creating.

When you embody the intuitive writing life, there's no final destination. Writing is — simply, naturally, and beautifully — a sustainable part of your life.

The magic is in the work.

You're writing.

You are a writer.

You're an intuitive writer.

GRATITUDE

To my friends, online writing community, and clients who bravely share their stories and writing adventures. Thank you for modeling surrender when you come to the page over and over.

To my editors and proofreaders for helping my voice shine throughout these pages.

For my God-given voice, gifts, and talents.

And, of course, to my husband and two kids, who support me and love me through everything I do.

THE INTUITIVE WRITING SCHOOL

Simplify the writing process...

An online space for creatives who want accountability, support, and authentic resources to write fast and write well.

I founded The Intuitive Writing School to help creative business owners sound human in their online copy and for writers to have the time and space to finish their creative projects.

While I initially created this resource for others, the community turned out to be what I needed to finish my first book. Then, I used the creative container to write and edit this book you're reading now. It was with the support, accountability, and butt-in-chair writing time with my community that I carved out the time and worked on this book.

Even though I supported entrepreneurs with their writing every day, my writing kept falling to the bottom of my to-do list — days and, eventually, months passed while projects sat untouched. I felt weighed down by all the words I wasn't putting on the page. When I realized I was thinking about writing more than actually writing, I recommitted and went all in on creating this space. Which really meant I was going all-in on myself.

The world needs your words too. Whatever writing project is on your heart, whatever story you need to tell, I invite you to join this sacred container and get the support you need to start — and finish. The words are already in you. Join us and let them out. Learn more and join us at jacquelinefisch.com/community

I'm excited to write with you,
Jacq xo

ABOUT THE AUTHOR

Jacqueline Fisch is an author, copywriter, writing coach, and founder of The Intuitive Writing School. She helps creatives move past writer's block and perfectionism so they can finish their important work, and she supports business owners in finding their authentic voice so they can make an impact on the world.

Before launching her writing and coaching business, Jacq spent 13 years working in corporate communications and management-consulting for clients including Fortune 500 companies and the US government. As a freelance copywriter and coach, she's helped hundreds of clients — tech startups, life and business coaches, creatives, and more — learn how to communicate more authentically and stand out in a busy online world.

After moving 14 times in 20 years, she's decided that home is where the people are. She finds home with her husband, two kids, two dogs, a cat, a few houseplants hanging on by a thread, and most of her sanity.

RESOURCES

Before you run off and think you need to read thirty more books on writing, a dozen books on the moon, and a few more on creativity – stop.

You just read enough. You are enough.

Before you start exploring more books, guides, and programs, promise you'll start writing, okay?

Do it for yourself.

For any resource you see here, know that this isn't an endorsement of a person or every piece of their work. Use your discernment, take what you can, and leave the rest. Here's a brief list of resources.

Books on language and writing

- *Frogs into Princes: Neuro Linguistic Programming* by Richard Bandler, John Grinder
- *Write. Publish. Market. 2nd Edition: From Idea to Published Book: The Entrepreneur's Blueprint* by Jodi Brandon

- *The Artist's Way* by Julia Cameron
- *The Right to Write: An Invitation and Initiation into the Writing Life* by Julia Cameron
- *Bird by Bird: Some Instructions on Writing and Life* by Anne Lamott
- *Still Writing: The Perils and Pleasures of a Creative Life* by Dani Shapiro
- *The INFJ Writer: Cracking the Creative Genius of the World's Rarest Type* by Lauren Sapala
- *All the Words: A Year of Reading About Writing* by Kristen Tate

Books on nature's rhythms

- *Moonology: Working with the Magic of Lunar Cycles* by Yasmin Boland
- *Women's Bodies, Women's Wisdom: Creating Physical and Emotional Health and Healing* by Christiane Northrup, M.D
- *WomanCode: Perfect Your Cycle, Amplify Your Fertility, Supercharge Your Sex Drive, and Become a Power Source* by Alisa Vitti

Books on self-improvement and spirituality

- *The Courage to Be Disliked: How to Free Yourself, Change Your Life, and Achieve Real Happiness* by Ichiro Kishimi and Fumitake Koga
- *Die Empty: Unleash Your Best Work Every Day* by Todd Henry
- *The Four Agreements: A Practical Guide to Personal Freedom* by Don Miguel Ruiz

- *Outrageous Openness: Letting the Divine Take the Lead* by Tosha Silver
- *The Surrender Experiment: My Journey into Life's Perfection* by Michael Singer
- *The Untethered Soul: The Journey Beyond Yourself* by Michael Singer
- *Zero Limits: The Secret Hawaiian System for Wealth, Health, Peace, and More* by Joe Vitale and Ihaleakala Hew Len

Find a complete list of resources to support your *Intuitive Writing* journey online at

jacquelinefisch.com/intuitive-writing-book

Made in the USA
Las Vegas, NV
02 June 2024

90629384R00184